AF485714

THE GOSPEL OF THOMAS

The Q source of Christianity

Book translated and commented by
Israël Nazir

ISBN : 9798818523835

MESSAGE FROM THE EDITOR

Salam, Shalom, Peace

The people of the Book or ahl al-Kitab in Arabic is a theological belief whose origin is found in the suras of the Koran. It is by this name that Muhammad, صاعس, the prophet of Islam, calls the Christian and Jewish communities living in the Arabian Peninsula in his time. He calls them such because they have access to a Book, it means the Tanakh for the Jewish communities and the Gospels for the Christian communities.

The interlocutors who listen to him in the marketplace of Mecca are Semites of Arabic language and tradition who have no Book to refer to and whose existentialist beliefs are based on a polytheistic pantheon with weak moral values. The inhabitants of Mecca see in these religious communities coming from abroad, an identity danger for their culture. This sentiment is becoming even more evident as more and more Arabs are converting to Christianity.

Muhammad, صاعس, received from his adoptive uncle a teaching in Syriac to the Christians of the Orient. He is a Quraysh caravaneer, i.e he is from the ruling tribe over Mecca and the Kaaba. He is in his forties and educated in the Jewish Tanakh. He presents himself to them as a messenger, who has come to communicate to them, orally and in Arabic, this precious knowledge that the People of the Book have, and to which they do not have access.

For doesn't it essentially say this:

"Each people on earth has received from God a messenger who came to teach them the teaching of Truth. Those who listened to him received a book and great wisdom, those who refused ended up forgotten and their remains are found in Syria and Egypt…"

The ahl al-Kitab editions, claim this origin and aim to continue the teaching of the Book to the inhabitants of Earth. The literary and theological definition of our Book is limited to the Dhammapada of Siddhartha Gautama called the enlightened Buddha, to the Proverbs of Solomon, son of David, king of Israel and Judah, builder of the temple, wise among the wises, to the Gospels of Jesus reported by Thomas, Matthew, Mark, Luke and John, to the Tao Te Ching of the old Master Lao-Tseu, to the Analects of Master Kong, latinized in Confucius, to the Bhagavad-Gita of Krishna, the all-attractive and to the Koran of Muhammad, صلعم.

The vision that drives us is not that of melting all religions into a single mould, nor that of mixing all traditions in a meaningless syncretism. In fact, we believe that when we study the Book, we realize that religions all speak of universal values that transcend identity beliefs and that these universal values speak of God, Peace, Virtue, Love, Harmony, Wisdom and Freedom.

We believe that when we study the Book, we

open up to the cultures of this world and that when we understand them, we can accept them. When one has accepted the traditions of this world, one obtains as a reward for this very great Wisdom: a profound serenity.

This is why we believe that each religious tradition is rich in unique teachings and that it carries within it, through its worship and its culture, a beauty that cannot be matched. We wish to define ourselves, to be like a stone sculptor who would leave aside his tools and who would be content only to polish the surface of the stone. Polish this stone as well as the 6 others:

"These 7 stones which contain the truth within and which form a whole of greater truth. A bigger building, a more coherent building. »

Our role is simple, it consists in allowing the exchange of knowledge between believers of different faiths and traditions. We want to do this in a theologically acceptable framework and we want to do it in an easy-to-understand format, and in as many languages as possible.

In this Book, which is at the foundation of all modern civilizations, we have found an ultimate Peace: a Peace with God, a Peace with oneself, a Peace with others. In this Book, we have found the answers to the existential debate which has animated human since his appearance. A debate which will animate eachone throughout his life:

Who are we? Where do we come from?

Where are we going?
What is Good? What is Evil?
Who is God?

Why believe in Him?
How to understand men?
What motivates them?
How to anticipate their actions?

Because in 2000 years, human has changed little, yet Humanity has evolved for the better. Isn't it, because human asks himself the essential questions from the beginning that Humanity has evolved for the better?

Why does Humanity ask itself these questions? It is because originally, everyone was wondering, that people appeared to answer...

In the teaching of these 7 ancestral sages, messengers of the Truth, you will undoubtedly find the best advice and the best answers.

Those who believe these are like us. We are the People of the Book: Ahl al-Kitab.

SOMMAIRE

PREFACE

The preface is interesting in that it unites in an instant the beginning and the end of the writing of this book. Because it is at the end of this long literary journey that I finally write what will be written at the beginning of this book. It is even more stimulating because I will address, in this preface, the main arguments which prove literary and historical that this collection of the Words of Jesus is authentic and that it is what modern historians call the Q source (Q is coming from Quelle, which means source in German).

According to Wikipedia, the Q Source or Document Q is a supposedly lost source which would be the origin of the elements common to the Gospels of Matthew, Mark and Luke. According to the hypothesis of historians, it is a collection of sayings of Jesus of Nazareth which would date from around the year 50. The Q Source hypothesis is a direct consequence of the theory of the two sources. The theory of the two sources being that the Gospel of Mark and the source Q serve as the source for the writing of the Gospels of Matthew and Luke.

Apart from its surprisingly complex mechanics, the two-source theory is of great benefit to historians, as it allows them to continue to argue that the Gospel of Mark is the first gospel that was written. In this, they oppose the Christian theological tradition which teaches that the canonical gospels were written in chronological order by Matthew, Mark, Luke and John. Modern historians base their interpretation on the historical fact that among the archaeological copies found, the oldest is a manuscript copy of the Gospel of Mark. They also argue that the Gospel of Mark is shorter than the other three and that the syntax used is simpler. Finally, they add that Mark uses Aramaic.

Before proposing further the arguments in favor of the thesis that I defend, I wish to present to modern historians some counter-arguments. First of all, the fact that the Gospel of Mark is found more easily, as well as the fact that it is shorter and simpler in expression, are to be related to the content of this Gospel and the success it obtained with his public... Because it must be understood that the Gospel of Mark is addressed to the Greeks and the Romans while the Gospel of Matthew is addressed to the Hebraic Jews. That is why the Gospel of Mark is freed from a too heavy Jewish culture. That's why it's shorter and simpler. That is why the symbolism conveyed by the miracles of Jesus reported by Mark is more convincing in the ears of the Greeks and Romans... Finally, the use of Aramaic by Mark occurs at the end of his book and these passages constitute above all the testimony of the life of Jesus to which Mark was really a witness...

If it were a question, as historians do, of simply classifying the Gospels chronologically by the number of pages they contain, then they should not doubt that the so-called "Gospel of Thomas" is even older... To those who would think that a modern approach is in essence closer to the truth than an ancient vision, I would point out to them that this debate is not new and that the thesis of this book is already found in the Koran of Muhammad , sAaws. In this book, the last prophet gives the following explanation: the gospels derive from a single original text which he calls the Injil.

The choice of the word Injil is also more appropriate, because it thus defines his paternity to the Evangiles or Gospels. To simplify and francize the debate on translations and linguistic appropriations, it must be understood that etymologically the name of the evangiles or gospels derives from the greek word angelos. "angelos" means in ancient Greek the message, while the prefix "ev" means good. What must be understood in the formation of this Christian neologism is that before the good versions of the message of Jesus, there was the Word of Jesus in a raw format.

This is the thesis that I defend in this book: Christianity does not derive from two literary sources, but derives from a single source Q, also called Injil or Angile, that is to say the so-called "Gospel of Thomas". This document does not date from the 50s, but dates from the first years following the death of Jesus and it then served as a source for the writing of the narrative Gospel of Matthew. Which narrative gospel then served, in chronological order, as a source for writing the Gospel of Mark, Luke and John.

Below are my 7 arguments in favor of the recognition of this book as the Q source or Injil:

1- During the foundation of each of the great religions of this world, we observe that there are only two types of foundation which represent the natural path of evolution of a religion. Religions are thus founded either by the verb or by writing. For example, Judaism, Hinduism and Taoism were founded by writings coming directly from the founders of their religions. Conversely, Buddhism, Confucianism and Islam were founded by the verb of their founders which was then transcribed in a raw format by the disciples and only thereafter were obtained explanatory, narrative and philosophical writings by successive authors.

In the case of Christianity, the Christian tradition seems to base its religion on the canonical gospels, but these texts, of great wealth, were not written by its founder and are not both rough transcriptions of the message of his founder. If we compare these texts with the religious texts of other religions, the canonical gospels are comparable to second generation writings. While the said "Gospel of Thomas" is comparable to the raw transcriptions of the religions founded by the verb. This intuition is also corroborated by the numerous indices of the New Testament which plead for a foundation of Christianity by the word of Jesus.

2- In the comments section, you will notice that we find traces of partial repetitions of the Word of Jesus among the authors of the New Testament. What is important in the study of these repetitions is that we see that this use is free and independent, some authors commonly use some logions while other authors have an exclusive use of other logions. The most striking example is that of Paul of Tarsus, who even makes a total and exclusive reproduction of a word of Jesus (logion 17). In the interesting case of Luke, we also note that these exclusive occasions are consistent with Christian chronology. Because its exclusive repetitions come from the end of the text whereas the authors of the New Testament who precede it mainly took up the words which are at the beginning and in the heart of the text.

Finally, what is remarkable in the use which is done with the Words of Jesus is that we see a free appropriation of the verb of Jesus which leads to a distortion of the original content. This is all the more convincing since it is a human mania for slightly distorting the original remarks and moreover the more the repetitions continue to be repeated, the more the distortions, additions or subtractions increase...

3- What I call root effect, is the effect of dilution of the original content in the development of Christian thought, whereas at the very beginning the Words of Jesus represented the whole of Christian thought, the more one advances in time, the more its concentration diminishes, the original seed has become a root, the roots have raised a tree above them, the tree is producing leaves, flowers and fruits. This progression is quite natural and this effect corresponds well with the use of a common source by successive authors. What is exciting about studying this book is that the more you study it, the more you realize that it behaves exactly as the original source should behave. And the root effect or dilution effect is an expected consequence of an original text, eroded by time. By making a simple statistical study of the partial or total repetitions of logions from this book in the New Testament, we obtain the following results: Matthew takes up 63% of the logions from this book, Mark takes up 30%, Luke 57%, John 24% and Paul 18%. Apart from Luke, who in his work represents a return to the use of Jesus's speech, we can clearly see the tendency towards a dilution of the use of speech by successive authors and publishers of Christian content. If we extrapolate with the usage of this book today among authors and publishers of Christian content, its usage must represent at best only a few percent of the total content generated each year.

4- Apart from behaving exactly as an original source would behave, this book also brings the missing link to the debate on the non-circumcision of Christians. Because according to the Christian tradition which is circumcised by the said "Gospel of Thomas", the non-circumcision of Christians is due to the epistles of Paul. However, if one looks at Paul's work with a neutral and external eye, it is really difficult to conceive how Paul, on his own and with only the use of a few sentences interspersed in his writings, could succeed in reversing a trend so deeply rooted among Jews and Judeo-Christians. This is all the more surprising since Paul is not a first generation disciple and his reception among the first Christians was so stormy that he had to be exfiltrated to Antioch. In truth, if Paul of Tarsus was able to convince the Christians on the subject of non-circumcision without suffering a strong challenge from the disciples of the first hour, it is quite simply because all the disciples knew very well that Jesus in his logion 53 had said that circumcision of the flesh is not useful.

5- The fact that this collection of the Words of Jesus behaves like the missing link is also found in the use that has been made of this book by slanderous and Gnostic authors. For Christian theologians, the fact that the so-called "Gospel of Thomas" is part of the main work of Gnostic literature is not in doubt and in this very uninstructive reading we find indeed traces of the themes, images and formulations specific to this collection of words. Concerning the slanderous authors, one finds in the logion 105 the proof of a use of this book as literary basis with the infamy… The fact that one finds partial or total repetitions of the said "Gospel of Thomas" in the three types of antinomic literature which are the canonical writings, the gnostic writings and the slanderous writings necessarily imply that the collection of words of Jesus was at the begining.

6- When we study in depth the 114 logions that make up this book, we quickly become convinced of their authenticity. Whether on the bottom or in the form, one is struck by the constancy and the coherence of the logions between them, which by the repetition testifies to the global vision of its author. To imagine that a writer would be capable of such coherence and consistency in the discourse of a literary character who is intellectually created, is more fiction than reality. Finally, the fact that most of the logions are taken up by the authors of the New

Testament demonstrates by the accumulation of official recognitions that these words are clearly authentic.

7- The seventh and last argument that I will use to argument this thesis is not rational, it would rather be defined as an emotional argument. This feeling that I call: attraction effect, is at the very origin of the writing of this book. While reading and studying this book, I felt drawn into a quest to find the origin of Christianity. This feeling is not unique to me, because it is also found in many authors who have studied this book and who also embark on a quest for meaning and a quest to Christian origin. If this attraction effect is so strong, it is because the contents of this book are truthful and authentic. That is why it draws us closer to Jesus living in the first century of the Christian era.

Finally, to conclude this preface, some, I hear them, will tell you what is the use of knowing the original word of Jesus, if the Fathers of the Church have decided to hide it to promote the good versions of the message of Jesus? This point of view is understandable, yet I perceive two notable objections. The first is that from a philosophical point of view, how can we know the end of the path when we do not know its starting point? Without the hindsight that is allowed by the knowledge of its origin, how can we orient ourselves in this labyrinth? It is crucial for orientation, but it is also decisive for accomplishing one's philosophical journey, because as often in life, the end of a journey is often only the return to its starting point... The second objection rhetoric comes from the historical analysis of its discovery. If destiny had seen fit to hide this book for eternity, then why does it reappear at a time when it is no longer possible to hide it?

To those who believe in destiny, listen to this true message, stop hiding the authenticity of this book and reclaim it. Because in this book, there is no heresy, it is the version of the word of Jesus which has everything in it to be recognized by believers of other traditions, as much as it has everything in it to be recognized by historians and secular people. So, do not be afraid, because the lost sheep I was, have found in this book the means to be definitively reconciled with Christianity. It is by getting closer to the historical and original Jesus that I found the means to make Peace. So do not be afraid, because many of us will follow this path that leads to reconciliation and peace with Christ.

"Those who follow Peace will always be well guided"

Salam, Shalom, Peace
Israel Nazir

PREFACE

BEFORE THE BOOK:
THE CONTEXT

Gustave Doré

PART 1
"The Essene Community"

The following story is a literary creation that is based on the testimony of the apostles and on historical facts. Through this story, we want to facilitate understanding and share a historical framework for learning. This fictionalized story is intended only to be instructive.

The setting of the life of Jesus was in roman times on the shores of the Mediterranean Sea. The colors of this decor are tinged with ochre, green and blue. These are the colors of the sun and the deserts, the lakes and the forests, the sky and the sea. Such are the landscapes of the kingdoms of Israel and Judea which were limited by Egypt and the Jordan. This original land which was still covered with lush vegetation is what the Jews call the promised land, what the Greeks called Palestine, what the Christians will call the holy land.

On the western bank of the Jordan River, we see in the distance a group of men advancing in procession towards the edge of the water. To the bugle of their trumpets and the hubbub of the men, they advance happily towards the long-awaited initiation rite. The man who is at the head of this morning procession, is called John-the-Baptist and he takes the men to the sands of a beach. At the water's edge, the young men sit while John the Baptist sinks into the calm waters of the river. Halfway up his body, he motions for one of them to come join him. Jesus gets up and goes to join John the Baptist in the coolness of the water. The sun illuminates the scene, while the movements of the fish and the chirping of the birds harmonize the place.

John-the-Baptist places his hands on the young man and says to him: "You have finally arrived at the gates of our community. You, Jesus, the son of Joseph and Mary, my relative, I observed you during your apprenticeship and I recognize in the adult: a pure among the pure. It is by the grace of your merit that you enter through this baptism into our great family. And before you receive the anointing of purity, come into my arms." The man grabs Jesus and turns him gently towards the living waters of the river.

When Jesus lifted his head from the waters and opened his eyes, he was dazzled by the Light. Coming from the beach, we heard shouts of joy and cries of surprise, because by a happy coincidence, a white dove had found itself caught by the wind of the river. It was frolicking in this current of air and yet seemed, to all eyes, to be standing fixedly above the heads of Its two men.

Coming out of the river, the men embraced their new brother and went back to the wooded hills overlooking the Dead Sea. According to the archaeological discoveries of the last decades, it is in this place that the soul of the Jewish community of the Essenes lived. According to the historian Flavius Josephus, there were among the Jews in Israel and Judea, three philosophical schools: the first had the Pharisees as followers, the second was that of the Sadducees priests and the third, which had John the

Baptist as leader practiced holiness and had taken the name Essene.

The Essenes were Jews by birth and had, according to the historian, a strong sense of affection that bound them together. They repudiated pleasures as a sin and held temperance and control of the passions as virtue. Despisers of wealth, they practiced a marvelous spirit of community. No one among them who surpasses the others in wealth, because among them one encounters neither the distress of poverty nor the vanity of wealth, but rather the pooling of the goods of each given for all. Living in sharing, the Essenes dressed in white with a band of linen at the waist. They regarded the oil of the Sadducees as filth.

The Essenes did not form a single city but lived scattered in large numbers in all the cities. When brothers arrived from another locality, the community put all its goods at their disposal to meet their basic needs. According to Flavius Josephus, their piety towards the divinity took particular forms, thus, before lunch, the Essenes wash their bodies with cold water and it is only after this purification that they gather in the refectory. They then take their places quietly and the baker serves them the communion bread. The priest pronounces a prayer before the meal and no one can taste it until the prayer has been said. Finally, according to the historian, they believed in the immortality of the soul and were fond of the teaching of the Book. They lived single, adopted orphans and disdained marriage...

In all likelihood with the writings of Flavius Josephus, Jesus became a member of the Jewish community of the Essenes and to be accepted there, he had to follow as an adult the examination of the elders for 3 years and only after having shown during this period that he knew how to behave properly, he could be recognized by the rite of baptism as a brother in the community.

After returning to the wooded hills surrounding the Dead Sea, Jesus set out on a journey through the Judean and Negev deserts. He wanted to take a step back and on this journey to an uncertain destination, he left accompanied by a Sicarii. The Sicarii were a Jewish community so named because of the "sica" dagger they wore in their belts. They prefer to be called zealots, because they see themselves according to the book of Maccabees as the fervent defenders of the Jews. Kept away from the cities by political power, they had formed a symbiotic relationship with the Essenes of the Dead Sea. The Sicarii brought their protection and in return the Essenes performed the daily tasks.

During this journey through the deserts, in search of the ancient kingdom of Solomon and the discovery of the Semitic faces that formed it, Jesus was confronted with hunger. To beg for a piece of bread, he gave alms and ate whatever was put in front of him. His travel companion had very harsh words during the journey. He was trying to convince Jesus to renounce his beliefs and join him in the exercise of hatred and violence. "These tribes, he said, are savages who have stolen our lands, we should hunt them and punish their sons so that they do not return." Jesus remained alert during the diatribes of the adversary and the only thing he allowed himself to tell him calmly was that according to the books of Moses, these peoples are the children of Shem, one of the sons of Noah. They are if you open your heart, your distant brothers and they are also those who feed us. The adversary laughed when he heard this and he replied: "You Essenes, you are hilarious, you see yourselves like doves, yet you look like pigeons! Don't you wish to become an eagle or a falcon? »

According to the Gospel of Matthew, Jesus resisted temptation in the desert. He then proceeded to the city of peace; it means: Jerusalem. From immemorial time, the holy city was a city made of stones and majesty. Based on the territory of the tribe of the benjamins, it is located at the intersection of the Jewish kingdoms of Israel and Judea. Since the times of Kings David and Solomon, it had become its political and religious centre.

Jesus enters the fortified old city through the Zion Gate and when he walks on its cobblestones, he remembers his childhood, when he ran in these alleys with his friends and his brothers. Mechanically, his steps transport him to the basin of Siloam and at the foot of this source of hygiene and freshness, Jesus washes his hands while raising his eyes towards the temple mount. His stomach tightens at the thought of climbing the steps and his hands shake at the thought of what he will see at the top.

The esplanade of the temple is rectangular in shape and at that time it was surrounded on these 4 lengths of porticoes which were used by the Jews as a courtyard. In the center of this terrace was, preceded by a square courtyard, the main temple of Judaism and in front of the courtyard of this central building, the Sadducees were doing their horrible tasks on the stone altar… Jesus looked with pain at the people bringing sacrificial animals. He looked with shame on those who claimed to be priests and who slaughtered innocent creatures in the name of God... In plain sight, the blood was slowly draining from the animal's neck. The beast was lying there, on its side on the ground, its tongue hanging out and its gaze lost... In their unpardonable errors, the Sadducees traded the divine indulgence for money: "With this money, they said, you can offer wood to burn or coat yourself with our fragrant oils to purify yourself. Jesus suffered watching them and in his heart he knew that he could not achieve peace with God, as long as these charlatans had control of His house…

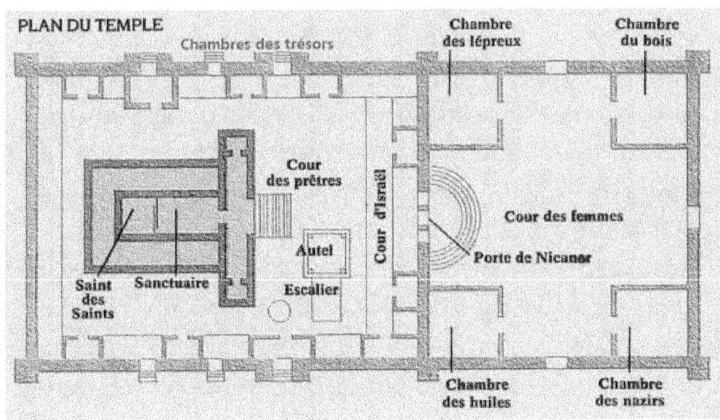

PLAN DU TEMPLE
Chambres des trésors
Chambre des lépreux
Chambre du bois
Cour des prêtres
Cour d'Israël
Cour des femmes
Autel
Porte de Nicanor
Escalier
Saint des Saints
Sanctuaire
Chambre des huiles
Chambre des nazirs

PART 2

"The Nazir of the Temple,
Melchizedek Forever »

After the horrific vision comes like fine weather, the comforting vision of Jesus walking to his native land of Galilee. On the way, he understands that there is something wrong in the Kingdom and it is surely, he thinks, because people have forgotten the word of the Eternal. Whether in Galilee or Samaria, whether in Decapolis or beyond the Jordan, he began to recite the words of the Lord. Standing in the market place or seated on the edge of a well, he stands with dignity in the midst of all and recites aloud the best chapters of Isaiah and Jeremiah, the songs of Solomon and the psalms of David, the Ketuvim and the Nevi'im.

The people who drank from his mouth were seduced by the eloquence and presence of this man and many were those who came to follow him. According to the testimony of the apostles, he was joined at that time by Simon called Peter and his brother Andrew as well as the sons of Zebedee John and James. From the four corners of Israel, admirers flocked and united around Jesus… Jesus spoke to them in parable of the Kingdom of God. He was talking to them about following the path of wisdom and holiness… He was talking to them in secret about Virtue, Love and Unity.

One day, while Jesus was reciting the proverbs of Solomon, people began to wonder if he had not become as wise as the great king of Israel and Judea, they wondered if he was not the son to whom Solomon had addressed his Book of Proverbs. In this Book, Solomon teaches his son the values that will allow his heir to maintain Unity in the Kingdom. And when Jesus recited the prophecies of Isaiah and Jeremiah, people kept comparing him. When they heard him reciting the Trei Assar of Zechariah and Joel, they asked Jesus, "Are you the one who was announced by the former prophets? Are you this offshoot of the holy root of David? The one called Nazar? »

Jesus remained unknown when asked if he was the Messiah they were waiting for. He preferred to talk about his universal message, because unlike the Essenes who addressed themselves only to Jewish men, educated and adults, Jesus opened the doors of the Kingdom to everyone: women and children were invited, the lost and foreigners were loved, the poor and the sick were educated and cared for. Jesus fed the world and people drank from his mouth.

He was residing in Galilee with his family when news came to him of the imprisonment of John the Baptist. The latter had been locked up by Herod Antipas, the tetrarch of Galilee and Perea. In Roman times, the kingdoms of Israel and Judea had been divided into several independent jurisdictions, each headed by a front ruler who ultimately owed his power to the Roman emperor. Herod Antipas was no exception and since he was a tetrarch, he believed that he could marry the wife of his living half-brother. John the Baptist was publicly offended by this, because according to the laws of Moses stated in the Torah, this was not permitted. John the Baptist said that because of this, the reign of Herod Antipas would suffer the curse. Then the cruel one locked John in prison and later executed him. The disciples of John the Baptist came to take his body and buried him.

On hearing the terrible news, Jesus, accompanied by his disciples and his brothers James, Simon, Jude and Joses, left Galilee by boat and headed to the soul of the Essene community. According to the Gospel of Luke, John the Baptist and Jesus were part of the same family and the Jewish tradition at the time gave a hereditary right of blood. This is why all eyes turned to Jesus when on the western mountain overlooking the Judean desert, he came before the entire brotherhood of the Essenes gathered, to take the oath to replace John the Baptist.

He said in front of everyone, to his brothers, his relatives and his disciples, that he would not behave like a master with absolute power, but that he would behave like a servant in the service of God and the community. That he would not dress in arrogance, smugness and disdain, but would behave with them as he had always done, that is to say with the feeling of affection that unites families: "You you are my brothers and my sisters. And what we do, we do for our Father who is in heaven. Those who walk in my way will bring unity and holiness into the Kingdom. We are neither usurpers* nor flatterers*. We are not in the service of the man of lies*... Such are unworthy to reign over the Kingdom. »

During his sermon on the mount, Jesus drawn attention and he convinced the community of the Essenes who acclaimed him in the name of Melchizedek i.e. in Hebrew: a righteous master... Jesus then went with his disciples to the regions around the Jordan to profess the good news of the coming of the Kingdom... According to the Gospel of Matthew, they met during this tour Pharisees who came to inquire about the message of Jesus and the behavior of his disciples. Having observed them, the Pharisees reproached the disciples of Jesus for not strictly observing the laws of Moses... To understand their criticisms, it is necessary to know that the Pharisees have a rigorous reading of the Tanakh and that he considers the Torah, i.e. i.e. the 5 books of Moses, as being the major teaching of the Book. It is in the in-depth study of these 5 books that they establish the rules to follow which define their identity belief.

In all likelihood with the content of his teaching, Jesus gave priority by right of posteriority to the Ketuvim and the Nevi'im. And in accordance with these two other subparts of the Tanakh, the mitzvahs of Moses had already been reduced by David, Isaiah, Micah, Amos and Habakkuk... Jesus sometimes professed to go even further... This theological position offended the most the Pharisee elites as much as it seduced many of them. They, the doctors of the Law, who had acquired through the synagogues the solid support of Jewish society. They felt threatened by the charisma and the verb of this Nazarene.

Seeing this discussion, the disciples understood the difficulty of the task and they began to doubt. One evening as they sat by the fire, they asked him about the future. Jesus answered them that by studying the book, we understand our past and that in it we find the secrets of our future… "Why do you doubt me? Don't you understand that as David received the anointing of the Samuel, I received the anointing of John the Baptist…? That as the shepherd of the tribe of Judah became king of Israel, I am the offspring of Galilee who is called: Melchizedek…? »

The disciples remained wary. Then Jesus gave them the parable of the strong man and after doubting, the disciples understood that he had a plan. His plan was simple and was inspired by the reign of Solomon, the builder of the temple. "We will make together the Yahad*, that is to say the great alliance, and when we will be strong, I will tear down this house and no one will be able to rebuild it! Hearing these last words, the disciples felt overwhelmed and in the morning the echoes of the Kingdom sounded in their heads.

They set off motivated in search of these new allies who would help them prepare for the coming of the Kingdom. Thanks to James-the-Just, they made a great alliance with the community of nazirs… The nazirs were another Jewish community which, to tell the truth, is rather a sum of individuals who are bound together by a vow of protection. They had no spiritual guide and referred to the Torah and the Book of Maccabees to develop a personal and religious cult around the body. Because, with them, the body is a holy temple and consecrated by a vow that cannot be touched by death... The contribution of the nazirs was important from a theological point of view and was also considerable from a political point of view. Because the Nazirs, reassured by the life nazireship of James-the-Just, represented a community comparable to the Essenes. According to the figures communicated by Flavius Josephus and the apostles, the nazir community was about 5000 men. The alliance now included 10,000 men and thanks to Simon-the-Zelot and Judas-the-Sicarii, the thousands were added. Thanks to Peter and Joses, the Galilean families of Tiberias and Nazareth accompanied them. Thanks to Phillip and Matthew, the Levites and Hellenists joined them. Thanks to Thaddaeus and Barthélemy, they reconnected with the Arabs of Nabathea and their wealthy caravaneers. Each of the 12 ministers brought a new member to this great new covenant.

While the disciples traveled the land in search of new allies, Jesus was at that time making the covenant of the heart with the Greeks, women and children. According to the Gospel of Luke, it was at this time that Mary-Magdelene, Mary-Salome, Joanna and Suzanne came to join him as disciples. The fire he had lit on Earth was spreading and all felt protected in his presence. The warmth of his love reassured them, and many of the misguided and unaffiliated came to join the grand alliance. They then began to believe with their hearts in the coming of the

Kingdom of God.

The disciples asked Jesus, "What are we going to do now that we have grown strong?" Jesus replied, "You know my word. We will go to Jerusalem to tie the hands of the usurpers. But we will do it in a pacifist way so that there are no deaths". The ministers then gathered the crowd of the grand alliance and they marched to the sound of goats' horns and the beating of drums, towards the aptly named Jerusalem. Arrived in front of the city, the crowd is positioned around the fortified city. On this Palm Sunday, Jesus enters the city welcomed as a king, he is acclaimed by the people in the name of the offspring of Galilee, ie. the Nazarene. According to the canonical gospels, the Jerusalemites waved palms as he passed.

Jesus then walks with great strides towards the temple of the Sadducees and when he arrives there, he chases away those who were trading there. Then he overturns the tables of the money changers and the seats of the sellers of sacrificial animals… Having noticed himself, he says to them: "It is written: My house shall be called a house of prayer. But you, you make it a den of thieves! Having said this, Jesus made himself a whip with the cords he had brought with him, and having tied them up, he promptly drove the merchants out of the temple. When they were driven out, he turned to the chief priests who were hiding or fleeing and told them: "You are usurpers! You are the heirs of Jason and Menelaus. The same people who supplanted the high priest Onias III for money offered to the powerful. Your worship is pagan! You are the shame of this House! The scribes who witnessed the scene were indignant at the things Jesus had done and they were shocked at the words he had spoken. Coming from the women's court, the children could be heard shouting: "Hosanna to the Son of David!" Welcome to you, heir of David! Please save us, son of David! »

*: these terms are taken from the Dead Sea Scrolls

PART 3
"The Eternal Covenant"

For several days, the Sadducees were heckled and reprimanded. By his presence, Jesus prevented their access to the temple and he taught the Cohens and the Levites. Jesus said to them, "Our father who is alive is a holy spirit, and those who blaspheme it will not be forgiven. The Lord looks with disgust at the horrors you are doing in His Name. Beware, because on the day of harvest the ryegrass will appear, it will be pulled up and burned!" During the day, the Sadducees hid and in the evening they were afraid that Jesus would come to their house and tie them up. They went to ask for support from the elders, scribes and Herodians. At the same time, far away on the Mediterranean coast sitting in Caesarea, Pontius Pilate, the Roman governor of the province of Judea, hears of the crowd movements, he organizes his legion and heads for Jerusalem.

"Hey, psst, did you hear the news? - Oh no, that's not true… He didn't do that! Jerusalem hummed with words and cooed with rumours. What seemed impossible before, today was shouting from the rooftops as the future. The long-awaited king had come and nothing could resist him. Nothing except the rich and powerful. The latter organized themselves and the city repeated it to the ears of the disciples. In the evening, they used to rest on the Mount of Olives. They spent their evenings there together making music and singing hymns. From up there, they had a superb view of the old town, the esplanade and the temple.

That evening the disciples shared their concerns with Jesus and Jesus answered them with the parable of Peace and the means of division. He spoke to them in mystery of the intergenerational fight that would bring Unity. The disciples were feverish and Judas the sicarius intervened: "Brother Jesus, tomorrow is the week of Passover which begins and as you know, according to tradition, it is forbidden for Jews in this place and at this time of year to fight or kill each other. Let's take advantage of the moment to take over the temple for good. Let's take advantage of this moment, when the crowd supports us and where the flatterer will be within our reach..."

Sensing that Judas' ardor was seducing the disciples, Jesus temporized and explained to them why he would refuse to do so: "By using force and violence to seize power, we would plant the seed of evil in the Kingdom. By not respecting the tradition of the Passover, we would put Moses and the Jewish people to shame. By defiling the temple on this holy day, we who proclaim the use of wisdom and holiness, we would lose our foundations. Judas, the land you wish to plow is not the good ground. Your desires possess you, your faith wavers! »

The next morning, which was the first day of unleavened bread, the disciples set about preparing the feast and the evening meal. During this time, Judas went to see the high priest Caiaphas and on the way that leads to meet him, Judas plagues in his heart of hearts: "The hour of the final fight* has arrived and the dove does not see it, he delays the moment when it is clear that it is the exact moment when, as it is written, the sons of Light will fight against the sons of darkness*. The pacifist is blind and foolish! I'm going to throw oil on the fire and whether he likes it or not, the final fight has begun..."

That evening, Jesus was in town and he sat down to table with the twelve. While they were eating, Jesus said, "Truly I tell you, one of you betrayed me..." The disciples were saddened when they heard this and looked at each other worriedly. Jesus then took bread, and after giving thanks, he broke it and gave it to the disciples, saying: "Take, eat, this is my body. Then he took a cup, and after giving thanks he gave it to them, saying, "Drink of it, all of you, for this is my blood, the blood of the covenant which is shed for many for the remission of sins...I tell you, I will not drink of the fruit of the vine until the day when I will drink it with you again, in the Kingdom of our Father. »

At the end of the evening, they went up to rest on the Mount of Olives. After a few hours, the disciples doze off and Jesus continues to pray alone. He stood solitary among the night birds that surrounded him with nocturnal anguish. He had a presentiment of imminent danger. To calm himself, he prayed our father, face down, and when he got up and bowed, he saw through branches the lights of the approaching torches. He recognized the voice of Judas, who came accompanied by Sadducees and elders to seize him. To the great surprise of the latter, Jesus allowed himself to be seized and he forbade the disciples to show violence. After his arrest, the disciples fled, except Simon Peter, who followed those who had seized Jesus. They went to Caiaphas, the high priest of the temple, in the courtyard of his house, the scribes and the elders were assembled in assembly to judge him.

In turn, the Sadducees presented their character witnesses who unanimously affirmed that they had heard Jesus blaspheme against the temple and blaspheme against the oneness of God. They accused him of sorcery, of seducing the people and leading them astray… Jesus remained silent for a time before this miserable spectacle before unleashing the thunder of his words: "Wretched Sadducees, your ignoble crimes have caught up with you. You slaughter the innocent creatures of the Eternal with impunity. Your worship is not dedicated to the holy of holies, but it is dedicated to the idols of money and death. Truly I say to you, from now on we will no longer eat your meat offered to idols. The high priest interrupted him and Jesus answered him. "You wish, Caiaphas, to know who I am? So I answer you: We are the children of the Light, the children of the Father and if you ask me who I am, then I tell you, straight in the eyes and well anchored in my sandals. I am His son." Hearing this, the high priest tore off his clothes and began to howl blasphemy. He cried so loudly that through the centuries and millennia we can still hear the roar of the fury of Caiaphas.

The next morning the Herodians joined in the trial. The Herodians were a sixth Jewish community that included the family and supporters of Herod Antipas. They feared Jesus because he questioned his leadership. After having held a council and agreed by majority that he should be put to death, they went to present him to Pontius Pilate. Because he was the only one who had the legal right to punish with death. Pontius Pilate listened to the laments of the Sadducees and Herodians and answered them: "The Roman Empire is centuries-old, the religion of nowadays romans is the imperial cult. The crime of blasphemy against your religion I cannot recognize in roman law. On the other hand, where our interests come together is in the capital crime of sedition. You tell me that this man calls himself the King of Jews and that he is inciting the Jews against the romans and their allies. This is sufficient to be liable to capital punishment. »

The governor's soldiers led Jesus into the courtroom and stripped him of his clothes. They covered him with a scarlet robe and they braided a crown of thorns, which they placed on his head. After doing this, they put a reed in his right hand. Then, kneeling before him, they mocked him, saying: "Hail to you, King of Jews!" And they spat at him, took the reed and beat him with it. Satisfied with their mockery, they took off his cloak, put his clothes on, and led him away to be crucified.

On the cobblestones, Jesus drags himself carrying the weight of the cross on his shoulder. Each step forward is a step towards the end of his ordeal. With a whiplash, the torturers guide him to the mount of the skull: Golgotha. On the western hill facing the temple mount, the soldiers crucify him, then they sit down, and guard him. To indicate the subject of his condemnation, they wrote above his head: "This is Jesus, the Nazarene, King of Jews."

A Roman soldier that afternoon took a spear and pierced the belly of Jesus. Before dying, Jesus gave his disciples his last instructions and told the inhabitants of Jerusalem who mocked him that he forgave them for having shed innocent blood during Holy Week. He forgave them for hurting him like Isaac had not. He forgave them for having killed him like a lamb...: "Let my sacrifice serve as a lesson to you and remove the speck from your eyes. From now on you will be able to judge for yourselves the quality of your leaders... Your eyes have seen, your ears have heard, your hands have touched, your hearts have been lifted up…I am now going to join my Father the living who is in heaven". And around the ninth hour, in a final gasp of agony, the spirit of Jesus flew away to join his Master.

According to the Synoptic Gospels, there were several women there who watched from afar and who had accompanied Jesus from Galilee to serve him. Among them were Mary Magdalene, Mary Salome and Mary, the mother of Jesus. When evening came, there came a rich man from Arimathea who named himself after his father and who was a disciple of Jesus. He went to Pontius Pilate and asked him for the body. Pilate ordered it to be handed over to him. Joseph took the body, wrapped it in a white shroud and carried it away.

Joseph brings the body to his family and during the first wake, the women still believed it... His body was still warm, they healed then his wounds and kept him warm. They accompanied him in death, prayed for him and asked him to return. The disciples also began to hope and accompanied them in prayer.

By the morning of the second day, the cold body had already begun to stiffen. The women understood the sign and at noon they announced it to the disciples. The news of Jesus' death had a devastating effect on the crowd and his family was left speechless when they felt the break in his body. The women began to cry and the pain plunged them into unhappiness. When injustice seizes your body and expresses itself in cries from the heart and tears of suffering... When the sadness of the loss of a loved one languishes in despair... Such was the second evening of the funeral wake of Jesus.

On the morning of the third day, the cold body of Jesus was whitish and the silence of death weighed down throughout the morning. Around noon, tongues began to loosen and it was agreed to bury him in the new sepulcher of Joseph which was carved into the rock. The disciples and loved ones sat that early afternoon in a circle around a sleeping Jesus who was lying on a stone in his white shroud. They took part in the calm and the sobs to offer him a last homage. Some had nice words, others asked to be forgiven. Nicodemus and Joseph took the body of Jesus and wrapped it in bandages and spices, as it was the custom of burial among the Jews. Then the body of Jesus was laid in his sepulchre, closed by a huge stone.

On the third evening of the wake, the disciples and relatives remained united despite the absence of Jesus. They spoke of the shame they felt and the injustice that tormented them: "We had the long-awaited Messiah, the righteous King who would reign over the twelve tribes of Israel but the sons of darkness stole him from us and now they hope that by his death, they will bury all that and then we will not speak of it again. They want us to believe that his way died with him. That, my brethren, is what gnaws at my heart…".

There was among the disciples, a disciple whose name was John and who was the disciple whom Jesus loved. As he heard his brother's lament, he looked at the stone on which Jesus had been lying and he saw a bird land on it to lay an olive twig on it. Turning to relatives and disciples, he said to them: "No, my brothers, Jesus is not dead. He is still alive and his word is still alive in us. They want to shut him up, well we'll talk about who he was. They want us to forget him, well we will write his word for eternity!" Hearing this, the disciples looked at each other convinced with eyes sparkling with life. After being tested, they had found and they begin to admire the idea...

Above them, perched on a branch in the trees, hung the bird that had followed them from the beginning and the story tells that this dove remained with the disciples thereafter. But that story is for after the Book that they sent down that night. This Book which is the authentic collection of the words of Jesus

Christ and which was handwritten in Aramaic by Jude named Thomas, the Twin.

Mater Dolorosa

La Pietà of Michelango

'In the beginning was the word, and the word was with God and the word was divine. »

**Gospel According to St. John
Verse 1 - Chapter 1**

THE GOSPEL OF THOMAS IN THEMATIC ORDER

Theme 1:
Logions about the Mysteries of Jesus, the Secrets of Knowledge

Here are the hidden words that the Jesus alive said, that were handwritten by Jude named Thomas, the Twin.

1. Jesus says:

"He who understands the meaning of these words will not taste death. »

2. Jesus says:

"Let him who seeks, do not cease seeking until he finds. When he finds, he will be tried. After being tested, he admire, he will reign over all.

5. Jesus says:

"Know what is before your face, and what is hidden will be revealed. There is nothing hidden that is sure to be revealed! »

6.

His disciples questioned him and asked:

"Do you want us to fast?
How should we pray?
Should we give alms?
Should we abstain from certain foods?

Jesus replies:

- Do not tell a lie, and what is loathsome, do not do it!
Everything is visible in the face of the sky. There is
nothing that is hidden that will not be discovered.
There is nothing covered that will not be revealed…"

7. Jesus says:

"Well guided is the lion that man will eat, the lion
became a man. Wretched is the man whom the lion
will eat, the lion will become like man. »

17. Jesus says:

"I will give you what no eye has seen. I will give you
what ears have never heard. I will give you what no
hand has ever touched. I'll give you what never
occurred to you."

29. Jesus says:

"If the flesh came into existence through the spirit,
that is wonderful. But if the spirit came into existence
through the body, it is a marvelous marvel.

I'm rather surprised by this:

How was this great wealth placed in this poverty? »

52.

His disciples said to him:

"Twenty-four prophets spoke in Israel and all expressed themselves through you. »

Jesus objects:

"You left the one living in your presence and you spoke of the dead. »

62. Jesus says:

"I tell my mysteries to those who are worthy of my secrets. Let your left hand ignore what your right hand is working out. »

67. Jesus says:

"He who knows everything, when he does not know himself, he is… deprived of everything. »

69. Jesus says:

" Well-guided are those who have been persecuted in their hearts. These are the ones in truth who have known the Father. Well-guided are those who are hungry, they can satisfy the stomach of whoever wants it. »

70. Jesus says:

"When it is begotten in you. It will save you. But if you don't have it in you. It will kill you. »

74. Jesus says:

"Lord, many are standing around the well, but there is no one to go down. »

92. Jesus says:

"Seek and you will find! The things about which you had asked me and which in those days I had not told you. Now I wish to tell you, but you no longer seek it.»

103. Jesus says:

"Well-guided is the man who knows when the thieves are coming. Let him watch and gather his wealth and family. Let him arm himself at the belt before they enter. »

108. Jesus says:

"Whoever drinks from my mouth will walk in my way. I too will become like him and what is hidden will be revealed to him. »

Theme 2:
Logions about the Kingdom of God

3. Jesus says:

"If those who guide you say:

'Behold, the Kingdom is in heaven!'
- Then the birds will be there before you.

If they tell you:

'Behold, the Kingdom is in the sea!'
– Then the fish will be there before you.

The Kingdom is inside of you and it is outside of you.

When you know yourselves, then they will recognize you, and you will realize that you are the sons of the living Father.

But if you don't know yourself, then you will be in poverty, you are poor. »

9. Jesus says:

"Behold, the sower came out
hand full of seeds to sow.

Some fell on the road,
the birds came and picked them.

Some fell on the rock.
They have not found where to sink their roots nor
have they managed to rise to the sky.

Others have fallen among the thorns who choked
them and the worm ate them.

Others finally fell on the good ground,
These brought forth an excellent fruit.

They gave sixty per measure. They gave up to one
hundred and twenty per measure. »

20. The disciples said to Jesus:

"Tell us what the Kingdom of Heaven looks like!

He answers them:

The Kingdom of Heaven is like a mustard seed, that
is, the smallest of all seeds.

When it falls on the plowed ground, it produces a
large stem which becomes a shelter for birds. »

40. Jesus says:

"A vine stock has been planted apart from the
Father. Since it is not strong, it will be torn from the
root and will perish…"

57. Jesus says:

"The Kingdom of the Father is like a man who has
good seeds to sow. At night his enemy came and
sowed ryegrass among the good seeds.

The man would not allow the ryegrass to be pulled
up, lest, he said, in taking the ryegrass you would take
away the wheat with them.

Indeed, on the day of harvest,
the ryegrass will appear,
we will tear them up and burn them! »

73. Jesus says:

"The harvest is plentiful. Few are the workers. Pray
to the Lord to send workers to harvest. »

76. Jesus says:

"The Kingdom of the Father is like a merchant who
owned a cargo. One day, he came across a pearl. This
trader was wise. He decided to sell all his merchandise
and buy this unique pearl for himself.

You too, seek for yourselves this treasure which lasts
and does not perish. Who resides where the moth
does not approach, where the worm does not gnaw. »

88. Jesus says:

"The angels come with the prophets to give you what
is yours.

Give them what you have and ask yourselves:

What day will they come to take what is theirs?"

94. Jesus says:

"He who seeks will find,
to whoever wishes to enter, the door will be opened. »

96. Jesus says:

"The Kingdom of the Father is like a woman who has
hidden a little leaven in her flour. The dough grows
slowly and will form beautiful loaves.

He who has ears to hear, let him hear! »

97. Jesus says:

"The Kingdom of the Father is like a woman who
bears a pot full of fruit. She goes along the path and
on the road, the handle of the vase breaks and the
fruits spill out behind her.

The woman does not know or care. When she got
home. She puts the vase down, turns it over and finds
it empty…"

107. Jesus says:

"The Kingdom is like a shepherd who had a hundred
sheep. One of them got lost. The shepherd left the
other ninety-nine and went after her until he found

her. After being tested, he said to the sheep: I love you more than the ninety-nine others. »

109. Jesus says:

"The Kingdom is like a man who has a hidden treasure in his field and yet does not know it.

He did not find it before he died, and he left his field to his son who also did not know that. He took the field and sold it.

The one who bought it, plowed the field and found the treasure. With this treasure, he began to lend at interest to whoever wants it. »

113. The disciples asked him:

"What will be the day of the coming of the Kingdom?

Jesus replies:

He does not come looking outward. People won't say look he's here, see he's over there.

The Kingdom of the Father is spreading over the earth and men do not see it. »

Theme 3:
Logions about fullness,
Absolute Unity, the Grand Alliance

4. Jesus says:

"The old man at the twilight of his life will not hesitate to question the child of seven days about the place of Life, and he will live!

For there are many first who will become last. They will return to oneness. »

16. Jesus says:

"Certainly men think that I have come to sow peace in the world. But they do not know that I have come to throw away the means of division: fire, sword and war.

If there are five in a house,
they will find themselves three against two and two against three, the father against the son and the sons against the fathers. They will rise united as one. »

18. The disciples said to Jesus:

"Tell us, how will our end come?

Jesus replies:

Have you already unveiled the beginning, so that you wonder about the end?

Where the beginning is, there will be the end.

Well-guided is the one who will stand in the
beginning, he will then know the end and he will not
taste death.»

22.

**Jesus saw little ones suckling
and he said to his disciples:**

"These little ones who suckle are like those who enter
the Kingdom.

The disciples asked him:

"If we are small (less), shall we enter the Kingdom?"

Jesus answers them:

"When you will make one with two, when you will do
inside as outside, when you will do the exterior as well
as the interior.

When you will make the top as well as the bottom
and the bottom as the top.

When you unite the masculine and the feminine. So
that what is not masculine becomes man. So that
what is not feminine becomes woman.

When you'll have eyes in your eyes,
a hand in your hand, a foot in your foot and a picture
in your picture. That's when you'll get in! »

23. Jesus says:

"I will choose you, one from a thousand and two from ten thousand and they will rise united as one! »

48. Jesus says:

"If two make peace in a house, when they say to the mountain: 'Go away!' then it will go away. »

49. Jesus says:

"Well-guided are you, the united and the chosen, because you will find the Kingdom.

You came from there and you will return there. »

89. Jesus says:

"Why do you only wash the outside of the cup?

Don't you understand then that he who created the outer side also created the inner side? »

106. Jesus says:

"When you unite the two into one, you will become the sons of men and if you say to the mountain, go away, then she will go away. »

114. Simon Peter says:

"Let Mary Magdalene come out of our midst, because women are not worthy of life.

Jesus says:

Listen, I will guide her so that she becomes a man.
Thus it will become a breath of life resembling to you,
the men.

Any woman who makes herself manly will enter the
Kingdom of Heaven. »

Theme 4:
Logions on Monotheism

8. Jesus says:

"The wise man is like a fisherman who throws his net into the sea. He brings up lots of small fish.

In the midst of these small fishes, he finds a large and excellent fish.

He throws the small fishes back into the sea and chooses the biggest without hesitation.

Let him who has ears to hear, hear! »

15. Jesus says:

"When you see the one who was not begotten of the female, prostrate yourself face down and adore him, for he is your Father! »

30. Jesus says:

"Where there are three gods, they are gods. Where there are two or one, I am with Him!"

32. Jesus says:

"A stronghold built on a high hill. Nothing can bring it down, nothing can hide it. »

44. Jesus says:

"Whoever slanders against the father, he will be forgiven.

Whoever slanders against the son, he will be forgiven.

But he who slanders against the spirit of holiness. This one, neither on earth nor in heaven, will be forgiven. »

47. Jesus says:

"It is not possible for a man to ride two horses. Nor is it possible for him to draw two bows. It is not possible for a servant to serve two masters, otherwise he would honor one and despise the other...

Never does a man drink old wine and immediately desire to drink new wine.

New wine is not poured into old wineskins lest they burst. Old wine is not poured into new skins, lest they spoil.

You do not sew an old piece on a new garment, because a tear would occur. »

59. Jesus says:

"Turn your eyes towards the Living, as long as you are alive. Dead you will seek to see Him and you will no longer be able. »

85. Jesus says:

"Adam came into existence from great power, great wealth.

Yet he was not deemed worthy of you. If he had been deemed worthy, he would not have tasted death. »

100.

They showed Jesus a gold coin stamped with Caesar's face and said to him:

"Caesar's men are asking us to pay their taxes.

Jesus replies:

Give Caesar what is Caesar's.
Give to God what is God's.
And what is mine, give it to me! »

Theme 5:
Logions about the Light

10. Jesus says:

"I have cast a fire on the world, and here I am watching over it until it spreads. »

11. Jesus says:

"This sky will pass, and he who is above him will pass away.

The dead have no life, the living have no death.

Today you eat dead things and make living ones.

When you're in the light, what will you do on that day?

You were in oneness then you became two, became two, what will you do? »

24. His disciples said to him:

"Instruct us where you are, for we must seek it! »

Jesus replies:

"Let him who has ears to hear, hear! If a light exists within a man of light, then that light illuminates the world. If he does not become light, what darkness! »

33. Jesus says:

"What you hear with your ears, teach it to others and shout it from the rooftops!

No one lights a lamp to put it on the bushel* nor does one put the lamp in a hidden place.

Rather, he places it on the candelabrum so that all who enter and leave see its light.

* Terracotta container that was used to store wheat.

50. Jesus says:

"If people ask you: where did you come into existence?

Tell them:

We came from the light, from the place where the light was born. He appeared in their image.

If you are asked: who are you?

Tell them:

We are his sons and we are the chosen of the living Father.

Finally, if they ask you what does it mean that the Father is in you?

Tell them:

It is movement and rest. »

77. Jesus says:

"I am the light that is above them all.

I am Everything. The whole came to me, the whole came out of me.

Split the wood, I'm here!
Lift a stone and you will find me there! »

82. Jesus says:

"He who is near me is near the fire. He who is far from me is far from the Kingdom. »

83. Jesus says:

"Images reveal something to man, but the light that is in these images is hidden.

In the image of the Father, the image will be hidden by the light…"

Theme 6:
Logions about the closed ones, ther relatives

12. The disciples said to Jesus:

"We know you will leave us.
Who will be great above us?

Jesus answers them:

At the point where you will be, you will go to James
the Just, it is for him that the earth and the sky were
created. »

21. Mary Magdalene asked Jesus:

"To whom are your disciples like? »

He replies:

"They are like little children who have entered a field
that does not belong to them.

When the owners of the field come,
they will say: "Leave our field! »

Then, like children, they take off their clothes, leave
the field and return it.

That's why I say:

"If the householder knows that the thief is coming,
he will watch before he comes and will not let him dig

an entrance into the house of his kingdom in order to take away his wealth

You too! Be vigilant in this world.

Gird your loins with great energy, so that the brigands do not find a way to reach you, because the profit you watch, they will find it!

Be aware and prepared!

Because when the fruit is ripe, he comes with his sickle to pick it…

Let him who has ears to hear, hear! »

25. Jesus says:

"Love your brother like your soul, watch over him like the apple of your eye. »

26. Jesus says:

"The speck that is in your brother's eye, you see it. But the beam that is in your eye, you do not see it!

When you have taken out the beam that is in your eye, then you will see how to remove the speck from your brother's eye. »

31. Jesus says:

"No one is a prophet in his village. No one is a
doctor for his relatives. »

55. Jesus says:

"He who does not renounce his father and his
mother cannot be my disciple. The one who does not
renounce his brother and his sister and who does not
take up his cross like me. This one will not become
worthy of me. »

61. Jesus says:

"Two will rest on a bed,
one will die, the other will live.

Marie-Salome questioned him:

Who are you, man?
Whose son are you?

You climbed on my bed and you shared my table, yet
I wonder.

Who are you, man?
Who were you born from?

Jesus replies:

I am the one who came from the one who remains
constant. I have been given what comes from my
Father.

Marie-Salome exclaimed:

I am your disciple!

So Jesus concludes:

"Because of this, I say this, when the disciple is open, he lets in the light and is filled with it. But when he is divided, he is filled with darkness. »

72. A man called out to Jesus:

"Speak to my brothers so that they share with me the property of my father.

Jesus replies:

Tell me, man, who made me a sharer?

He turned to his disciples and says:

Am I really a divider? »

79.

In the crowd, a woman called out to Jesus and said to him:

"Blessed is the belly that carried you.
Blessed is the breast that fed you!

Jesus replies:

"Blessed are those who have heard the word of the Father and who keep it!

Truly, the days will come when you will say:

Blessed were the days when this womb had not given birth, Blessed were the days when these breasts had not nursed.

99. The disciples said to him:

"Outside are your brothers and your mother!"

Jesus replies:

You and those who do my Father's will, these are my brothers and my mother. They are the ones who will enter my Father's kingdom. »

101. Jesus says:

"He who does not renounce his father and his mother, as I did. This one cannot become my disciple. The one who does not love his father and his mother, as I did. This one cannot become my disciple.

Because my mother gave me a body to die, but my true mother gave me life. »

105. Jesus says:

"He who knows his father and his mother, would they call him the son of a prostitute? »

Theme 7:
Logons on the Savior

13. Jesus said to his disciples:

"Compare me. Tell me who I am like. »

Simon Peter says:

"You are like a righteous angel. »

Matthew says:

"You are like a wise and philosophical man. »

Thomas says to him:

"Master, who are you like...?
My mouth can't grasp it. »

Jesus replies:

"I am not your master, because you have been
drinking. You have satiated yourselves at the gushing
spring of which I have taken the measure…"

Then he grabbed Thomas and they pulled away.
Then he said three words to him.

When Thomas returned to his companions, they
questioned him:

"What did Jesus tell you? »

Thomas answered them:

"If I said one word to you that he said to me, you would pick up stones and stone me. A fire would come out of it and you would burn!

14. Jesus says to them:

"When you fast, you will beget sin for yourselves. When you pray, they will condemn you. When you give alms, you will do harm to your spirits...

When you go into a country and walk through the countryside, if they welcome you, eat what they put before you.

And those who are sick in those places, heal them! What goes into your mouth will not defile you, but what comes out of your mouth will defile you! »

28. Jesus says:

"I stood in the midst of the world and in the flesh I manifested myself to them. I found them all drunk and I found none thirsty.

My soul is grieved over the children of men. Because they are blind in their heart and do not see why they came into the world. Empty, they came into the world, without anything, they will leave it...

May someone come and straighten them up, because here they are staggering! When they have slept off their wine, they will repent. »

37. His disciples asked him:

"When will you manifest yourself to us?
When will we see you? »

Jesus replies:

"When you undress shamelessly and trample your
clothes like little children do. Then you will see the
Son of the Living One and you will no longer be
afraid. »

38. Jesus says:

"Many times, have you longed to hear the words I
speak to you. And there is no one else you will be able
to hear them from. The days will come when you
look for me and will not find me.

43. His disciples called out to him:

"Who are you, you who tell us these things? »

Jesus replies:

"By the things I tell you,
don't you recognize who I am?

You are like some Judeans
who love the tree and hate its fruit,
who love the fruit and hate its tree…"

51. His disciples asked him:

"When will the day of rest for the dead come?
When will the day of the advent of the new world
come? »

Jesus answers them:

"What you expect has already happened and yet you
did not recognize it. »

66. Jesus says:

"Show me the stone that the builders rejected. This is
the cornerstone. »

91. They said to him:

"Tell us who you are, so that we believe in you."

Jesus replies:

You scrutinize the aspect of sky and earth, but the
one in front of you you do not recognize. This
present moment you do not know how to interpret. »

111. Jesus says:

"The skies and the earth will roll up before you, and
he who lives of the living will not see death.

That is why I say: he who finds himself, the world is
not worthy of him. »

Theme 8:
Sayings about the resting place, Paradise

19. Jesus says:

"Well-guided is he who was before he became!

If you become my disciples and listen to my words,
these will serve you like stones.

There are five trees in Paradise which change neither
summer nor winter. Their leaves never fall.

Whoever knows them will not taste death! »

42. Jesus says:

"Come into being as you pass away. »

60.

Seeing a Samaritan carrying a lamb entering Judea,
Jesus asked his disciples about the lamb.

The disciples said to him:

"He will kill it and eat it! »

Jesus replies:

"As long as it is alive, he will not eat it. Only if he kills
the lamb, he can eat its corpse. »

The disciples remarked:

"For no other reason would he hurt him!" »

So Jesus concludes:

"You too! Seek the Place of Rest, so that you do not become corpses, so that you are not eaten. »

68. Jesus says:

"Well-guided are those who are hated and persecuted. Those who persecute them will not find the place where they will not be persecuted. »

75. Jesus says:

"Many stand before the door, but it is the bachelors who will enter the bridal chamber.

86. Jesus says:

"Foxes have dens. Birds have nests. Yet the son of man has no place on earth to lay his head and rest. »

90. Jesus says:

"Come to me, my yoke* is just! Sweet is my authority and you will find (eternal) rest for yourself. »

* The yoke is a piece of wood that is put on the heads of oxen in order to hitch them up and guide them.

Theme 9:
Logions on Asceticism

27. Jesus says:

"If you don't fast from this world then you won't find the Kingdom. If you don't make the Sabbath the Sabbath, you won't see the Father. »

36. Jesus says:

"Do not worry from evening to morning or from morning to evening, what clothes you will wear. »

46. Jesus says:

"From Adam to John the Baptist among those begotten of women there is none greater than John the Baptist.

It is because his vision is right that it is said that his eyes will not be broken!

That's why I say:

"Whoever among you will become small (less), that one will know the Kingdom and he will be above John the Baptist."

54. Jesus says:

"Well-guided are the poors, the Kingdom of Heaven is for you. »

56. Jesus says:

"He who has understood the world, finds a corpse. He who found this corpse, the world is no longer worthy of him! »

80. Jesus says:

"He who understood this world, found the body. He who found this body, for him, this world is no longer worthy. »

81. Jesus says:

"He who has become rich, let him become king, and he who has power, let him give it up. ".

84. Jesus says:

"For whole days you stare at your reflection and rejoice. But, when you see your models, those who came into existence long before you, those who no longer die and no longer manifest.

How long will you endure it? »

87. Jesus says:

"Wretched is the body that depends on another body. Unhappy is the soul that depends on these two. »

95. Jesus says:

"If you have money, do not lend it with interest, but give it to he who has nothing in his hands. »

104. They said:

"Come, let us pray and fast today.

Jesus replies:

What is this sin that I have committed?
How did they conquer me?

It is when the spouse has left the marital room that it is necessary to fast and pray. »

110. Jesus says:

"He who has found the world and made himself rich, let him renounce this world. »

112. Jesus says:

"Wretched is the flesh that depends on the soul.
Wretched is the soul that depends on the flesh. »

Theme 10:
Logions against the elite, the rich and the powerful

34. Jesus says:

"If a blind man leads another blind man, both will fall into a pit. »

35. Jesus says:

"It is not possible for anyone to take a strong man's house by force without first binding his hands, only then can he plunder his house. »

39. Jesus says:

"The Pharisees and the scribes took the keys of knowledge and hid them.

They did not dare to open the door and they did not let others enter.

But you, know how cunning is the serpent but stay pure like the dove. »

41. Jesus says:

"He who has in his hand, it will be given to him. But he who does not have, even the little he has, it will be taken away. »

45. Jesus says:

"We don't harvest grapes from brambles. Nor are figs picked from the thistles. This is because they do not produce fruit!

The good man brings good things out of his attic. The evil man draws from his attic, which is none other than his heart, evil things and from his mouth come out horrors.

From the abundance of the heart, he does bad things.»

53. His disciples asked him:

"Is circumcision useful or not?

Jesus answers them:

If circumcision was useful then their fathers would have begot them circumcised from their mothers…

But true circumcision, that of the spirit, is totally profitable. »

58. Jesus says:

"Well-guided is the man who has been tried in his life, for he has entered into life. »

63. Jesus says:

"There was a rich man who had a lot of wealth. He thought of using his fortune to sow the fields. And when the harvest comes, he thought to himself, my barns will be full and I won't want for anything.

That same night he died.

Let him who has ears to hear, hear! »

64. Jesus says:

"A man had guests, and when he had prepared the feast, he sent his servant to call those guests.

The servant went to the first guest and told him that his master was inviting him.

He answered him:

"I have money for merchants and they are coming to my house tonight and I have orders to place. I apologize for the feast. »

The servant then went to another guest and told him that his master was calling him.

He answered him:

"I bought a house and it will take me all day. I am not free today, I apologize to your master. »

The servant then went to another guest and told him that his master was calling him.

He answered him:

"My friend is getting married, and I am preparing the feast. Sorry, I couldn't come. »

The servant then went to the last guest and told him that his master was waiting for him.

He answered him:

"I bought a field, and I have not yet gone to collect my share. I apologize for the feast, but I couldn't come. »

The servant returned and told his master that those whom he had invited to the feast had apologized.

The master then said to his servant:

"Go out into the streets, and whoever you find, bring them to me for dinner. Buyers and merchants will not enter my Father's house. »

65. Jesus says:

"A man of integrity had a vineyard which he had given to farmers to work on it and receive from them the fruit.

He sent his servant for the cultivators to give him the fruit of the vineyard. They seized his servant, struck him and nearly killed him.

The servant returned and told his master. His master thought, maybe they didn't recognize him?
So he sent another servant. This one also the cultivators struck him.

So the master sent his son, saying to himself that perhaps they would be ashamed to behave in this way with his child.

But, when the growers knew that this one was the heir to the vineyard.

They seized him and killed him.

Let him who has ears to hear, hear! »

71. Jesus says:

"I will tear down this house, and no one can rebuild it. »

78. Jesus says:

"What are your reasons for walking in the countryside? Is it to see a reed shaken by the wind? Or is it to observe a man wrapped in rich fabrics?

The kings and the powerful may wear beautiful clothes on them, nevertheless they do not know the truth! »

93.

"Don't give what is holy to dogs or it will end up like manure. Do not throw the pearls to the pigs, lest they make… *"

*The word is incomplete on the Coptic manuscript.

98. Jesus says:

"The Kingdom of the Father is like a man who wants to kill a powerful man.

In his house, he draws the sword and sticks it in a wall. Once he has ensured that his hand is steady, he kills the man of power. »

102. Jesus says:

"Woe to them, woe to these Pharisees!

They look like a dog lying down in the manger of oxen. He neither eats this food nor does he let the oxen eat it. »

END

After the book
The Apostolic Age

PART 1
"Apostles and Martyrs"

On the first day of the week following the Sabbath, Mary-Magdelene and Mary-Salome went early in the morning to the sepulcher carved in the rock. They had taken with them herbs and perfumes of myrrh to embrace one last time the loved one who had left them. When they arrived in front of the holy sepulchre, they were extremely surprised by the fact that the stone in front of the tomb had been turned over and when they entered the open tomb, they did not find the body of the one they were looking for. What amazed them greatly was that the bandages that had been used to wrap Jesus were scattered on the ground, while his white shroud was folded and laid aside. The myrophore women then ran to announce to Simon-Peter and John what they had seen and what they presented.

In those memorial days and in the weeks that followed, the wildest rumors swirled above Jerusalem and flew to the shores of Tiberias in Galilee. Some said that the Sadducees had taken away the body of Jesus to make it disappear. Others recounted having heard from the disciples that Jesus had risen from the dead and that they had seen and even touched him in his stronghold in Galilee.

The Sadducees, who had thought by their infamy to break the great covenant, now found themselves haunted in their nights by the mystical figure of Jesus prowling the Earth... The disciples, on the contrary, grew in faith and in prestige and they affirmed themselves in public as the representatives of the new holy and eternal covenant. They told the Jews who gathered around them, under the porticoes of the esplanade of the temple, that Jesus had become for them: "the Just King who would lead them forever. For the nobility of his death demonstrates the justice of his government. Thanks to his sacrifice, there was no death. His word is the source of life and it will live on through us. He has sent down the saintly spirit upon us and we will continue to serve him. »

According to the Acts of the Apostles, in those days Peter arose in the midst of the brethren, and the number of those assembled being about one hundred and twenty. He said to them: "My brothers, the prophecies which are written in the Book had to be fulfilled... The betrayal of Judas had been predicted and Jesus himself had prophesied it. He who was our brother betrayed us. He, who was counted among us and who had part in the ministry, this one made a mistake in his choices... He was seduced by Satan and devoured by shame and remorse, he hung himself on a tree... In the Psalms, David said in speaking of the adversary: let his days be few... Let another take his charge..."

The disciples therefore met in Jerusalem in the upper room where they usually sat. The eleven disciples were Simon surnamed Peter, John and James the sons of Zébédée, Andrew the brother of Peter,

Philippe the former disciple of John-the-Baptist, Thomas the Didyme, Barthélemy surnamed Nathanaël, Matthew the Lévi, James-the-Just, Simon-the-Zelot and Jude surnamed Thaddaeus. They were surrounded by women and by Mary, the mother of Jesus. They presented two postulants: Joses-the-Juste, brother of Jesus and Matthias. The disciples made this prayer: "Lord, you who know the hearts of all, designate which of these two you have chosen, that he may share in this ministry and in this apostolate". Once the prayer was over, they drew lots, and the lot fell on Matthias who was associated with the eleven apostles.

During the weeks following Matthias' appointment, the disciples continued to distribute oral and written copies of the words of Jesus in Aramaic. On the day of Pentecost, while there were Jews staying in Jerusalem who lived abroad and who did not speak Aramaic, the disciples decided to inform them by translating the teaching of Jesus into ancient Greek. and in Hebrew. The people watching the disciples trying their best at speaking foreign languages did not understand what they were doing and began to believe that they had become drunk.

Faced with this hubbub of incipient discontent, Simon-Peter spoke during a famous speech which is transcribed in the Acts of the Apostles. Thanks to this speech, Peter managed to convince many people among the Hellenized Jews who came to Jerusalem from Egypt or Turkey, in the direction of Syria or Mesopotamia. The latter were called by the Hebrew Jews, the Hellenists because they had learned the Tanakh in ancient Greek and lived in the former empire of Alexander the Great. In those days after Pentecost, many accepted to recognize Jesus and those who remained were baptized by the disciples. According to Luke the Evangelist, the community increased to about three thousand souls.

The new arrivals persevered in the teaching of the disciples and in the Essene fellowship. They repeated the breaking of the bread during the day and they recited their prayers in the evening. To enter the community, they sold their properties and their goods and they shared the product among all, according to the needs of each one. The community had everything in common and they lived together in the same place.

According to the Word of Jesus, the first Christian community was entrusted to James-the-Juste. To him the government, because "it is for him that heaven and earth were created". Made, by the word of Jesus, the heir to the Kingdom, James-the-Just accomplished a long mandate of about thirty years in Jerusalem and during his celestial mandate, he made wise decisions to ensure living together. The first of these important decisions was to center the posterity of Jesus on the values of a family that is part of a community united in a church. In the symbolic vision of James-the-Just, the Kingdom became the community and the temple of purity became the body of the bishop. And since James the Just was a Nazir for life, believers knew that in his hands the temple in Jerusalem would be protected from the death of the impious.

The nazirs who had been incorporated into the alliance continued all their life to see in James-the-Just a spiritual guide and they embraced with joy this new life which brought them meaning. They, the solitaries who lived outside of a sense of community, welcomed this rebirth with open arms into a new life that revolved around a family that kept the values of asceticism and sharing. It was with bitterness that the zealots learned from the mouth of James-the-Just that the sicarii were henceforth excluded from the alliance. Those who remained therefore had to remove the knife and from that day on, the sicariis harbored the regret of having been excluded from the saintly and eternal covenant.

After Pentecost, Andrew, the brother of Simon-Peter, was the first apostle called to go far away to preach the teachings of Jesus. He left with copies in Greek, Hebrew and Aramaic. And during his trip, he told those who frequented him the words of Jesus and who he was. According to Christian tradition, Andrew accomplishes his apostolic mission all around the coasts of the Black Sea. His travels led him to go through Mesopotamia and then go up to Turkey to the coasts of the Black Sea. Then he skirted them westward to the Bosphorus, descended along the coast of the Aegean Sea before taking a boat for Attica in Greece…

According to the Acts of the Apostles, in the weeks that followed Andrew's departure, Peter and John went one day to the temple to convince the Jews of Jerusalem and they said to them: "Repent therefore and convert yourselves, so that your sins be blotted out. For Moses said, The Lord your God will raise up for you a prophet like me from among your brothers. You will listen to him in everything he tells you and whoever does not listen to this prophet will be exterminated from among the people... All the prophets who have successively spoken, since Samuel, have also announced those days... So, listen! You are the sons of the prophets and of the covenant that God made with our fathers. All the families of the earth will be blessed in his posterity and it is to you first that God has sent his servant to bless you, so that he will turn you away from iniquity. »

A few days later, while Peter and John were talking at the temple, the priests came accompanied by the commander of the temple and some Sadducees. Anna, the high priest and her brothers Caiaphas, John, and Alexander were present. All who were of the race of the chief priests were dissatisfied with what they taught the people. They laid hands on them and threw them in prison. The next morning, the leaders of the people, the elders and the scribes, assembled in Jerusalem, and after threatening Peter and John, they forbade them to speak and teach in the name of Jesus.

Peter and John reported the news to the disciples and together they shared their sense of pride in feeling worthy of Jesus. They then decided during the weeks that followed to continue to teach the Word of Jesus and to continue to tell the Jews who he was... Then the usurpers laid their hands on the apostles a second time and threw them into public prison… Fortunately, the good people of Jerusalem supported the disciples in their fight and an angel of the Lord, having opened the doors of the prison during the night, brought them out, and said to them: "Go, stand in the temple, and announce to the populates all the words of this life. »

The apostles therefore entered in the morning into the temple, and they began to teach. The high priest was warned that the disciples were teaching in the temple and he sent the officers to check the prison. These tell him: "We found the prison carefully closed, and the guards who were in front of the doors, but, after opening, we found no one inside". Then the priests again summoned the Sanhedrin and all the elders of the sons of Israel, and they decided to send the commander of the temple to bring back with the guards and the ushers, the disciples of Jesus. The commandant and the officers seized the disciples and led them away without violence, for they feared being stoned by the people.

After they had brought them into the presence of the Sanhedrin, the high priest questioned them, according to Luke, in these terms: "Did we not expressly forbid you to teach in this name? And behold, you have filled Jerusalem with your teaching and you want to bring down on us the blood of this man! Peter and the apostles replied, "We must obey God rather than men." The God of our fathers raised Jesus whom you killed. God raised him up by his right hand as prince and savior, to give Israel repentance and forgiveness of sins. We are witnesses to these things, as well as the saintly spirit, whom God has given to those who obey him. ". The Sadducees did not know what to answer and a Pharisee, named Gamaliel, doctor of the law, esteemed by all the people, rose in the Sanhedrin, and he ordered the apostles to leave for a moment. Then he addressed the congregation and said to them, "Now I say to you, do not concern yourself with these men any more. Let them go, because if this company or this book comes from men then it will destroy itself. But if it comes from God, you cannot destroy it. So do not run the risk of having fought against God. »

The congregation agreed with the Pharisee, and having called the apostles, they had them beaten with rods. They then forbade them to speak in the name of Jesus and then released them. The apostles withdrew from before the Sanhedrin, rejoicing that they had been counted worthy to be insulted for the name of Jesus. And every day, in the temple and in the homes, they did not stop teaching and announcing the good news of Jesus Christ.

Faced with a strong growth of the community, the twelve decided, as much to promote the teaching of Jesus as to solve daily problems of food management of a large community, to put in charge below them a group of 7 Jews hellenists. They thus elected Stephen, Philippe, Prochore, Nicanor, Timon, Parménas, and Nicolas to office. The apostles, after praying, laid hands on the deacons to give them the saintly spirit and then gave them Greek copies of the Word of Jesus. The 7 deacons carried out the daily tasks and began like 7 trumpets of Jericho to prophesy on the meaning of these Words.

Their talent succeeded in seducing people and thanks to them, a large part of the priests obeyed the Christian faith. One day as Stephen stood before a crowd of Hellenists and argued over the prophetic meaning of Jesus' Words, men in the crowd grew indignant and accused him of speaking blasphemies against the temple and against Moses. They succeeded in moving the people, the elders and the scribes and they presented his case before the Sanhedrin. During his judgment before the Jewish assembly, testimonies confirmed that he had heard him say that Jesus, this Nazarene, will destroy this place, and that he will change the customs that Moses gave. Then Stephen proved himself worthy of the words of Jesus, he stood firmly before the Sanhedrin and he confirmed to them that they had heard the future correctly! Then they uttered loud cries, covering their ears, and they all rushed at him together. They dragged him out of the city and, having surrounded him against a wall, they stoned him with stones... Thus died Saint-Stephen, the first Christian martyr. Luke relates that witnesses laid his clothes at the feet of a young man named Saul.

Gustave Doré

PART 2
"The Man of Lies"

Before we go further into the history of the apostolic age, we are going to go back in time and tell you about a historical figure who, despite appearances, happens to be an important actor in history. This man is the one that the first Christians called the man of lies and history tells that when he laid his hands on Jerusalem, he did not come in person to seize it, but that he found servants to monopolize it… Because in the years which followed his accession to power, he bamboozled the flatterer who thought through the man of lies to have access to a greater power…

According to book XV of Jewish Antiquities by Flavius Josephus, it was at this time that the king of Judea, Herod I, became more and more distant from national customs and by the introduction of foreign customs undermined the ancient constitution which maintained the people in piety. For the glory of Caesar, the flattering king instituted games which were to be celebrated every four years. As improvements, the King of Judea had a vast amphitheater and a hippodrome built outside Jerusalem. He brought in athletes and competitors of all kinds from everywhere, attracted by the victory and the prizes offered, because large rewards were offered not only to sports athletes and charioteers, but also to musicians and gymnasts.

All the research of luxury and magnificence were deployed by Herod to give festivals which put in relief its greatness. All around the theater were arranged inscriptions in honor of Caesar, trophies recalling the peoples he had vanquished and conquered, all executed in pure gold and silver. As for the material, there were no expensive clothes or precious stones which were not given the spectacle at the same time as that of the games. Ferocious beasts were brought in, lions in large numbers, as well as other animals chosen from among the strongest and rarest... They were made to tear each other apart or fight with the condemned.

Flavius Josephus relates that foreigners were struck with admiration by the sumptuousness deployed, at the same time as keenly interested in the dangers of this spectacle. The Jews, who were indignant, saw in this the certain ruin of the customs in honor among them. Because, in their opinion, this spectacle was of manifest impiety. To throw men to beasts for the pleasure that other men find in looking at it is ungodly morals. And this the Pharisees who are doctors of the Law also recognized. But, above all, what saddened them were the trophies... Because the Pharisee masters saw them as idols. However, for the guardians of the ark of the covenant who have received the teaching of Moses, there is no greater error than having idolatrous morals...

History tells that from the beginning of the empire, the man of lies set up the imperial cult. To establish it, he deified his adoptive uncle with the title of Emperor Caesar and he built places of offering and sacrifice to his glory. He explained to the Romans that Caesar being the master on Earth, he was now their new deity. His heir, that is to say himself, therefore had the divine mandate to govern. Under cover of modernity and empire, he wrote the biggest lie in history.

Herod maintained skilful and cordial relations with him and he seized opportunities to flatter him. In order to shower his master with gifts, he built in his honor the city of Caesarea on the Mediterranean coast. In the center of the city, facing the port and on a hill, Herod built a temple for the imperial cult. Thus the navigators could see in the distance the temple of Caesar, which contained inside the statues of Rome and the emperor… As a reward for his compromise, Herod received the government over new territories in the North. Following the death of Zenodorus, he received Galilee and all the surrounding region.

Despite the appearance of his diplomatic successes, Herod was actually in a very unpleasant position. Because the people were unhappy and many resented the definitive introduction of these new beliefs. They saw in this the ruin of piety and the decadence of morals. This was the very subject of all the conversations of the people who were subject to irritation and trouble. Herod, being of a suspicious nature, closely watched this state of mind and to stifle the dispute and secure his hold, he acted in three stages: first, he decided to lower taxes, then he undertook the reconstruction in Jerusalem of the temple. Finally and above all, he tightened the security screw very tightly and he suppressed all possible occasions for agitation, obliging the inhabitants to always be at their work, forbidding all meetings to the townspeople as well as walks and visits.

The man of lies heard that his servant built other temples than those he had built to his glory. So when the rebuilding of the temple of Jerusalem was completed, he commanded Herod to do two things in order to demonstrate his submission to him. First, he should lock up in a contingent Roman building of the temple and under the guard of Roman soldiers, the vestments of the high priests. They will therefore have to present themselves to the Romans to be able to receive their clothing and they will also have to return them at the end of their office. Then, the man of lies ordered Herod to hang on the pediment of the main gate of the temple esplanade, a huge golden eagle. The message that the man of lies was passing on at that time was crystal clear. In imperial worship, the bird of prey symbolizes Caesar, the divine protector of kings... The Pharisees, who are clairvoyant, recognized the worship of the golden calf, this cult that Moses had forbidden in the past!

The continuation and the end of the reign were for Herod a long series of sufferings and corruptions. The subject of the succession of the kingdom of Judea poisoned the spirits. It is sometimes said that parents have the children they deserve, it is often true, because children imitate their fathers. Herod to access the throne had not hesitated to kill his brothers to take power and at the end of his reign when he felt threatened by his sons, he did not hesitate to kill them. The king of Judea finally died of illness and after his death, the man of lies led the succession and to better reign he decided to divide the kingdom between the three remaining sons: to Archelaus he gave Judea, Samaria and Idumea, to Herod Antipas he gave Galilee and Perea and to Phillip he gave management over the Decapolis. To their great regret, none of them received the title of king.

In the times surrounding the succession of Herod appeared Judas the Galilean. This brave man was at the head of a protest movement which, according to Flavius Josephus, was at the origin of the sicariis. The object of this protest movement was to remove the golden eagle that hung from the temple door, and for 10 years after Herod's death, the rebellion undermined the authority of Archelaus. In the year 6 AD, the man of lies, annoyed by the dangers posed by the sicarii on his precious eagle, decided to defeat Archelaus and incorporate Judea into the Roman Empire. He then appointed Coponius as prefect and the latter put an end by arms to the revolt of Judas the Galilean.

7 years later, when Jesus was a 13-year-old teenager, the man of lies died and on his tomb worthy of a pharaoh, he had engraved in stone: here lies ~~the emperor Caesar, son of god, Octave Augustus~~… The news went around the Mediterranean and ushered in the impious age when for centuries the roman emperors compared themselves to living gods who had to be honored in their temples with offerings and sacrifices… In truth, the History will demonstrate it, to the roman emperors the temporary government on Earth and to the righteous king the Eternal Kingdom

of Heaven, to men of lies: cruelty, violence and darkness and to Jesus: goodness, Wisdom and Light.

The succession of the empire had been prepared before his death by the man of lies and to ensure its continuity, he had adopted as his son the next Caesar. Around the 20s AD, that is to say at least 6 years after the new emperor came to power, Herod Antipas, seeking to flatter him, had a city built in his name on Lake Galilee. This city is still called Tiberias today. Herod Antipas followed in this the monstrosities of his brother Phillip who had built near the cave of Pan on the Golan Heights, the city of Caesarea Panias. In this city, which the Jews mockingly called Caesarea Phillipe, a pagan cult was devoted to a half-man, half-goat chimera...

In the year 26 AD, Pontius Pilate was appointed governor of Judea and within weeks of his inauguration, he took his army from Caesarea on the Mediterranean coast to establish it in Jerusalem during winter quarters. Pontius Pilate had the idea to make himself pleasant to his master to introduce effigies of the emperor into the city. The Jews protested ardently against his representations and despite Pontius Pilate's death threats, they remained together steadfast in their demands. After a week of conflict, Pontius Pilate backed down and brought the emperor's effigies to Caesarea. There, to make himself forgotten, the roman governor built a sanctuary in honor of the emperor, which he named the Tiberium.

The roman historian Tacitus wrote in his Annals that Emperor Tiberius behaved like a tyrant who encouraged denunciation as a system. He rewarded informers and employed them to preach falsehood... last years of his government are described by the roman historian as dark years, where one could be judged for simply speaking ill of the emperor. It was just needed to find someone to testify... His death occurred in 37 AD, on the island of Capri where he lived the last years of his reign in exile. He died of suffocation by Quintus Naevius Sutorius a.k.a Macro and after his cremation, his ashes will be deposited in Rome, under the hubbub of the Romans, in the august mausoleum of the man of lies.

To situate ourselves in the chronology of the apostolic age, this moment corresponds to the period which surrounds the death of the first Christian martyr i.e. Saint-Stephen. At the time, the early Christian church was shaken by prophetic interpretations of the Word of Jesus. These Essene prophecies greatly shock the Pharisees who support the Sadducees in the martyrdom of Saint Stephen. The Sadduceho-Pharisee repression then extended to all the members of the communities gathered in the primitive church of James-the-Just, it concerned above all those who repeated these prohibitions orally. According to the Acts of the Apostles, all except the apostles dispersed into the regions of Judea and Samaria.

Among the members of this movement orchestrated by the Sadducees high priests was a Jew from the tribe of Benjamin, whose name was Saul. The Pharisee entered the houses to snatch the men from their wives and throw them into prison. When he was done with Jerusalem, they sent him to Damascus in Syria to hunt them down. On the road to Damascus, Saul recounts in his epistles to the Galatians that he had a supernatural revelation as he fell to the ground and lost consciousness. For a moment outside of time and space, he encountered Jesus who urged him to cease his persecutions. On arriving in Damascus, Saul approached the Christian communities and was baptized by Ananias of Damascus. From then on, he took the name of Paul and for the next three years he preached the teaching of Jesus in Syria and Arabia.

At the same time, Philip, one of the 7 Hellenist deacons, was in Samaria and according to Luke, he was preaching Christ to the Samaritans. The Samaritans are a religious community that dissociated itself very early from Judaism on the questions of the book to be recognized and on the location of the Temple. For the Samaritans, this one should have been in Samaria while for the others, the temple is located in Jerusalem. Because of this, they were looked down upon by the Sadducees and Pharisees. When Philip came to meet them, the Samaritan crowds were attentive to his words and thanks to his message, many women and men were baptized.

The apostles who were in Jerusalem, having heard that the Samaritans were being baptized, sent Peter and John to investigate. When they arrived, the two apostles prayed for them to receive the saintly spirit. Because they had only been baptized by Philip. Peter and John therefore laid hands on them, and they received the saintly spirit. When Simon the magician saw that the saintly spirit was given by the laying on of hands of the apostles, he offered them money to obtain it. This behavior greatly angered Pierre who publicly reprimanded him.

This event is important for Christian theology, because it considers that Simon the magician is at the origin of the misinterpretations of the words of Jesus. These bad interpretations will be excluded from the official canon at the end of the 2nd century by the Fathers of the Church and they are still nowadays awkwardly called apocryphal gospels, awkwardly because these titles come from ancient Greek and mean in English the good hidden word.

When Peter and John returned to Jerusalem, they told the other apostles what had happened and from that moment began to concretely ask themselves the question of the correct understanding of Jesus' words. The copies made by Thomas spread well and the apostles recognized in these words: the saintly spirit. Although convinced by the message, they did not see the Hebrew Jews becoming so and they perceived in the openness towards the Samaritans and the Hellenists the dangers represented by a misinterpretation of the words of Jesus. At that time, therefore, the primitive Church found itself attacked from all sides: internally by the preludes to a syncretic Gnosticism and externally by a regal Phariseeism.

In a gesture of appeasement towards the Pharisees; James the Just argued that the house Jesus spoke of was his body and that as long as he was alive the temple in Jerusalem would have nothing to fear.

As for the subject of circumcision and by extension of the laws of Moses, the Jews must always under his mandate continue to respect the indispensable…

In the midst of all this debate comes unexpectedly Paul of Damascus. Although the apostles are reassured of his conversion by Bartholomew, they remain distant. Luc says that it is with Pierre that he makes himself heard. Paul, had been instructed in Wisdom and Virtue by Gamaliel the Pharisee and although he had not received the teaching of Jesus during his lifetime, he recognized the saintly spirit in his word. From then on, he said to the disciples: "To convince the Hebrew Jews, it would be necessary to develop a writing similar to that used by our ancestors in the Book. We should keep their symbolic and apological styles in order to put Jesus on the level of Abraham or Moses. This is how you will find the means to convince them. Because the Pharisees will not be persuaded by the misinterpretations of the Hellenists. For the Jews to believe in it, it will be necessary to make the word of Jesus, his gospel."

After careful consideration, the apostles accepted his proposal and Paul was asked to provide a text of this quality. Paul accepted his apostolic mission with honor and temperance and wrote the Epistle to the Hebrews. In all likelihood with the content of this epistle, his message was greeted with irritation by the Jews of Jerusalem who already saw in Paul a traitor to the Pharisees. The Hellenists, who had been chilled by his return, took advantage of the situation to take revenge. They sought, as Luke would write, "to take his life." Paul was warned in time and was then exfiltrated out of Jerusalem. This is how he found himself going to preach the message of Jesus, in his native land of Tarsus, in the city of Antioch in Turkey.

Despite these events, his epistle was a source of inspiration for the three columns of the church in Jerusalem represented by Peter, John and James-the-Juste. They discussed it among apostles and they agreed to write a gospel for the Hebrews coming directly from the Twelve. This task was entrusted to Matthew, because, being a Levi, he had a good knowledge of the Tanakh. As for James-the-Just, as he was the brother of Jesus, he was commissioned to write about his birth. This gospel was most warmly received by the Jews of Jerusalem. Thanks to the author of course, but also thanks to the narrative quality of the work.

Peter then left Jerusalem and went to preach the gospel to the Jews who lived on the Mediterranean coast in Jaffa and Lod. At that time, Pierre realizes that thanks to his experience and his charisma, he is able to convince some of the Jews. Through the gospel, he manages to build bridges with them. He goes up the Mediterranean coast to the north and then arrives in Caesarea, there, he understands, following the conversion of Corneille who is a centurion in the oman legion, that he has in his hands the means to bring down the man of lies...

At the time, the emperor was called in English: tiny toes, that is to say in Latin: Caligula. The roman emperor Tiny-toes was surely one of the worst men of lies who reigned on Earth. And that is surely why his reign was so short. It is said that his megalomania was matched only by the madness of his cruel pleasures. According to the roman historian Suetonius, more than 160,000 animals were sacrificed to inaugurate his reign... To thank Macro for his services, he ordered him to commit suicide with his wife. Tiny-toes would surely have preferred that this one refuse, because he could thus indulge in his perverse pleasure of cutting off heads. His madness led him to order that in all the temples of the empire, whatever their cults, a statue representing him as a deity be installed. There was unrest and riots everywhere. In Alexandria in Egypt, the Jews rose up against the roman governor, because this order also concerned their synagogues. On January 24, 41, Tiny toes was assassinated by members of his imperial guard. His ashes will be buried in the august mausoleum of the man of lies.

PART 3
"Prophecy Fulfilled"

During the almost 30 last years that make up this last part of the apostolic age, we will witness the crossings in a precise time and place of 3 historical groundswells. The first with which we will begin concerns the Christian advent and its internationalization.

Following the example of Andrew, the first called, the apostles left Jerusalem one after another to go and preach the gospel to the peoples of the earth. Among the apostles were mainly the twelve disciples of Jesus. John, the disciple whom Jesus loved, thus left the Holy Land at the same time as Peter and after a long journey across land and sea, he went to settle on the shores of the Aegean Sea in Ephesus in Turkey. On the spot, John organizes like James-the-Just in Jerusalem, a church of faithful, then he begins to write. With a real talent, John will participate as an author in the literary and theological boom that accompanied the writing of the Gospel of Matthew. According to Christian tradition, the son of Zebedee is the author of 3 eponymous epistles which he published in Ephesus as well as a canonical gospel. Finally, John is the author of the book that concludes the New Testament, a book he wrote on the evening of his long and austere life on the island of Patmos: the book of revelation : the Apocalypse.

Andrew, Peter, Paul, Phillipe, Matthew and John were also accompanied in their apostolates by

Thomas, the copyist of the Angile, who left with Barthélemy nicknamed Nathanaël and with Jude called Thaddaeus, towards the kingdom of Edessa in Syria. At the gates of the desert, the 3 former ministers of Jesus will succeed in converting the king of Edessa to Christianity. According to Christian oral tradition, the 3 apostles originated the preaching of Greater Armenia, i.e.: the first Christian kingdom. On the borders of Armenia and Persia, the 3 apostles separated. Jude, the brother of Jesus, continued to enter Armenia, while Bartholomew and Thomas left for the city of Nineveh on the Tigris River. After preaching to Jews and foreigners, the two apostles of the Aramaeans went to established churches on the coast of the Indian continent.

Simon-the-Zealot, for his concern, left to preach with Matthias who had replaced Judas in his ministry, towards the southern regions of Jerusalem. They preached together the good version of Jesus' words in Judea and then Matthias left to continue his journey to Egypt while the zealot plunged into Arab lands. On the shores of the Red Sea, Simon converts Berbers then he returns to the wooded hills that surround the Dead Sea in search of his brother Jude called Thaddaeus.

The only one who remained in the city of Peace was James-the-Just, the founder of the primitive church of Jerusalem. In Nazirite worship, the nazir's body and saintly spirit represented the new temple of the community. He was then meant to stay in Jerusalem. In his sermons, he promised the Jews who joined them in the path of Jesus to live together a new life of sharing and love, a life that would lead them to the place of eternal Rest, Paradise.

For nearly three decades and thanks to the holy life of James-the-Just, the Christian church was able to grow in safety in Jerusalem. Thanks to the means of the Gospel, Christian thought was developing strongly internationally, and Jerusalem heard with surprise about the waves of conversion abroad. This adherence to the Christian movement was gradually taking root among some of the Jews and flourishing among the uncircumcised. The incorporation of the uncircumcised into the Nazirite cult of the circumcised Jews of Jerusalem was accompanied, as is the nature of men, with misunderstandings about the practice of the cult and difficulties in choosing a name that would federate the movement.

According to the author of the Acts of the Apostles, these debates gave birth, in Antioch, to the name of Christian. That is to say those who recognize in Jesus the Christ: a term which means the one who had received the divine anointing to govern the Kingdom. The title is actually a anglicization of the Greek word chrestos, which translates the term mashia'h מָשִׁיחַ in Hebrew.

The worship debates that agitated the Christian movement are transcribable in the New Testament epistles written by Paul, James, Peter, John, and Jude. They are also transcribed historically by Luke in the Acts of the Apostles. These theological debates will be at the origin of an intense Christian literature of which will be part the pseudo-Christian literature found in 1945 in Nag-Hammadi, in Egypt. This pseudo-Christian current of Gnostic thought developed independently of the church in Jerusalem and their teachings were based on their own interpretations of the Angile of Thomas. Without landmarks with the aptly named, they wandered off in search of universalism in the shameful fields of a syncretic vision that has, for his reader, no cultic or theological sense.

Finally, to conclude this first historical groundswell, we will talk about the last two authors of the New Testament. They are Mark and Luke, the authors of the eponymous canonical gospels.

John called Mark was a Hellenized Jew who resided in Jerusalem when Jesus was welcomed as a king on Palm Sunday. He then witnessed the last earthly days of Jesus. Through his eyes, Mark experienced the via dolorosa of Jesus on the cobblestones. He suffered during the crucifixion on Mount Golgotha and this unexpected encounter with Jesus definitively changed the destiny of the young man, because in the days and weeks that followed, he went to see Peter to learn more... Peter recognized the young man and succeeded in convince him to join them in the way of Jesus.

The arrival of Mark in the church of Jerusalem was immediately a significant contribution for its members, because John surnamed Marc was a rich man and to enter the community, it was necessary to abandon its goods and wealth to give them to the bishop of the community, i.e. in the case at James-the-Juste. Having sole control of the property, the bishop would use it to meet the basic needs of church members.

As Mark came from a very wealthy Jewish family whose businesses and homes were scattered between their native shores of Libya, Egypt and Jerusalem, Mark had received an education in history and writing in Greek and Hebrew. His talent was then used by the authors of the epistles to correct and translate their writings.

Mark then followed Peter, when the latter went to Antioch to visit the new Christian church that Paul had founded. He then became familiar with the egalitarian functioning set up between circumcised and uncircumcised. There he met Luke and then he accompanied Paul and Barnabas in their apostolic missions through ancient Greece and its many islands.

We still do not know even today the precise date of the writing of his canonical gospel and to tell the truth, the debate still agitates contemporary historians who establish the writing of the gospel according to Mark before the gospel according to Matthew. According to Christian tradition, the Gospel of Mark was written after that of Matthew. And from a religious and theological point of view, its affiliation with the Gospel of Matthew seems more coherent with the evolution of Christian thought. Starting from the Angile to end up with an Evangile/Gospel for the Hebrews, the Gospel of

Mark presents itself rather as a gospel for the Romans.

This point also corroborates History which tells that during the last part of his life, Mark took with Peter and Paul the direction of the Roman Church. From a literary point of view, the fact that he takes care to take up the historical framework of Matthew, and the fact that he keeps a symbolic and apological style, prove that his writing follows that of Matthew. By his unique and confirming testimony, Mark opened the door to the compilation of the New Testament.

Finally, concerning Luke, who is the author of a canonical gospel and the Acts of the Apostles, we have kept very little information about his life. Sign of a very Christian humility, the writer spoke little or nothing about himself in his books, he recounts in an apological style the events of which he was the spectator and what was said during these days. Accurate theologian, Luke was a Hellenized Jew from Syria who had joined Paul in the management of the church of Antioch.

The Christian tradition situates the writing of its gospel after that of Mark and its gospel constitutes the return to the use of the words of Jesus contained in the Angile. By the use he makes of it, Luke confirms the authenticity of the original message contained in the said Gospel of Thomas and he also confirms the canonical Gospels of Matthew and Mark.

The second historical groundswell that constitutes this last part of the apostolic age is that of the cycles of persecution against the disciples of Jesus and his apostles. In this horror show, painful to write, we always find the same actors in the roles of executioners and victims. We find again the usurpers, the flatterers and… the man of lies.

According to the dating circulating among historians, it was in 44 A.D. that the Christian martyrs continued. On this date, the murder is the decision of the last king of Judea, Herod Agrippa, who slew one of the Twelve with the sword. Herod Agrippa had received the mandate to govern thanks to his successive relations with the emperors Caligula and Claudius. He reigned over a large territory that stretched from the Golan Heights to the Judean Desert. He saw himself as the king of the Jews and watched with jealousy the successes of Christians Abroad. To assuage his frustrations, he had an amphitheater built in Beirut in which gladiator fights took place. According to Flavius Josephus, to organize the fighting, he designated all the criminals he had, in order to punish them while making a spectacle of war a peaceful celebration. He had all these men killed down to the last... Luke wrote soberly in the Acts of the Apostles: "King Herod began to mistreat some members of the Church and he put to death with the sword: James, the brother of John, Apostle of Jesus. »

Then came the martyrdom of Jude called Thaddaeus. The one who ordered the murder of the apostle was none other than the man of lies. He who covered himself in Rome with the glory of having conquered England and of having annexed Judea felt disturbed by the news coming from the East which announced that the Christians were converting the kings of the former Partho-Armenian empire. However, the man of lies wished to extend his influence over these vassal kingdoms and when he heard that Jude called Thaddaeus was going to marry the daughter of the great king of Armenia, he personally intervened with the renegade to remind him that the cult to convert on Earth was the imperial cult... Faced with the pressure coming from the absolute master on Earth, the great king of Armenia submitted and he ordered in Makou, in the north of the country, the execution of his daughter Sandoukht and her husband Jude called Thaddaeus.

After the martyrdom of Jude Thaddaeus, Bartholomw also called Nathanael, took over the supervision of the Christian community of Edessa and Armenia. Later, Bartholomew will be executed on the orders of a flattering king in Artaxata, the Armenian capital. According to Armenian tradition, when he was put to death Bartholomew was flayed alive, crucified and beheaded.

In this painting which is lugubrious, which is brushed with blackness and splashed with red, which illuminates the reflections of a blade of bronze. The most deserving will suffer persecution before dying as a martyr. This is the case of Peter and Paul, who will suffer many persecutions that led them to the gates of death. These trials brought them closer to Jesus, because they felt worthy to suffer persecutions like him. Jesus, they knew, had gone all the way, and the two apostles will do the same.

Before dying, Paul suffered the persecution of the usurpers in Jerusalem. According to historians, it was at Pentecost in AD 58 that Paul made his public return to Jerusalem. The atmosphere in the city was electric and the discontent of the townspeople perceptible. Much time had certainly passed, but that was not enough for the Jews who had not forgotten his epistle to the Hebrews. They had also heard the news about his speeches and actions against the practice of circumcision. Arriving in town, Paul goes first to Mark's house to meet with James-the-Just.

James welcomes Paul with a greeting of peace and says to him: "Shalom Paul, you are back when perhaps it would have been better if you hadn't come back. The situation is dangerous for your life, I advise you to make your request as soon as possible to place yourself under the status of the nazirs, because as you know, during your nazireship no Pharisee or Sadducee will risk killing you. Redouble your vigilance, because there are assassins on the prowl. Take four nazirs brothers with you to protect you. I can organize this for you, but you will still have to take care of feeding them. Paul listened silently and replied that he would follow his advice. James-the-Juste added: "In fact, I must tell you, here it is as I wrote it and as we agreed. We have decided not to impose any charges other than these, which are indispensable. We abstain from meat immolated to idols, from blood, from strangled flesh and from illegitimate unions. You would do well to keep it. Farewell."

The next morning, Paul enters the temple accompanied by his brothers to announce the day on which the purification would be accomplished and the offering presented for each of them. Before the ceremony of nazirship took place, the Jews of Asia, having seen Paul in the temple, stirred up the whole crowd, and laid hands on him, crying: "Men of Israel, help! Here is the man who preaches everywhere and to everyone against the people, against the law and against this place."

By the term against the law, one must understand against the Tanakh, by the idea of a thought against the Tanakh, one must understand against the Torah, by the book of the Torah, one must understand that Paul speaks against the laws of Moses. When Paul allows the uncircumcised Christians of Antioch to remain uncircumcised and when he bases his decision on the Word of Jesus, Paul, according to his detractors, is preaching against the Law.

Paul was then seized by the temple guards and the roman cohort to be tried before the Jews and the Sanhedrin. He was so presented before King Agrippa II. Paul, it seems, had a joker up his sleeve and before being condemned to death, he publicly revealed to the Jews that he was a roman citizen and that therefore no Jewish, religious or monarchical authority had the power to condemn him to death. Constrained by roman law, Paul was sent by King Agrippa II to

Rome to stand trial. Arrived in Rome, there is no doubt that no roman magistrate would ever have given his consent to apply Jewish regulations to a roman citizen.

Persecutions against Christians peaked in AD 62. That year, the Christian church was decimated twice. Andrew was crucified under Emperor Nero at Patras in the northern Peloponnese. While James-the-Just was killed by the Sadducees high priests who accused him of transgressing the law. According to Flavius Josephus, James-the-Juste died stoned after being thrown from the esplanade of the temple.

His death extremely shocked the Jewish opinion which saw in this misdeed a sacrilege. Because, by doing this, the Sadducees were demonstrating to everyone that even the high priests did not respect the laws of Moses. Because of this, the Sadducees lost all credit in the eyes of everyone. The Jews therefore refrained from frequenting the temple and increasingly turned to the synagogues and churches for prayer, singing and study. The place became so sad that Flavius Josephus says that to run the shop, the Sadducees allowed foreigners to sacrifice in this place...

The last martyrs that took place before the fateful year of 70 AD were those of Peter, Paul and Thomas. Peter and Paul will be arbitrarily devoured by hungry beasts during games organized by Emperor Nero in Rome. Thomas the copyist will end up in India, murdered with a spear in the back while praying in a cave in Mylapore, near Madras.

These events finally bring us to the last part of this story, which ends with the last historical groundswell that crossed the road of persecution and Christian advent. This groundswell is that which concerns the word that Jesus had said at the beginning.

It was in the summer of 66 that the time came when the usurpers of the temple of Jerusalem paid the price for their crimes and their injustices. The divorce between the Jews and the Sadducees was consummated when they saw the Sadducees sacrificing animals for the romans in honor of Caesar. It was when they saw them defile the stone altar in front of the temple that there was no turning back between the Jews and the old philosophical school.

Those who put an end to the abuses of the Sadducees were the Sicariis who enjoyed the popular support of Jews and Judeo-Christians. The Sicariis had one main objective and they had been fighting for it for almost 80 years. In the days of Judas-the-Galilean, they had been within an inch of achieving it, in the days of Jesus, they had even been within a hand of achieving it. For more than 30 years, the Sicarii had found themselves within an arm's length of being able to touch this imperial eagle which adorned the main door of the esplanade of the temple. This lie visible like a gash on the face of Jerusalem.

It was Menahem, the third son of Judas-le-Galilean who, watching for opportunities, waited for the opportune situation, 4 years after the sacrilege of James-the-Juste, during the end of Nero's reign,

Menahem launched the revolt and seizes by force the fortress of Masada held by the romans. They thus recover the weapons and the leader of the insurrection rushes with his troops towards Jerusalem. They crossed without hindrance the fortifications at the entrance of the city and attacked, near the temple mount, the roman garrison of the fortress of Antonia. After these two victories, Menahem permanently removes the golden eagle from the main door of the temple and refuses to return the Sadducees to their high priests' outfits, by doing this he prevents the Sadducees from officiating in their ignominies. Seeing this, the Jerusalemites acclaim the sicarius like a king. During his enthronement in the city, he presents himself as the comforter, that is to say in Hebrew: Menahem.

By his liberating action, Menahem convinces the Jews to free themselves from the yoke of the romans and their allies. By his request for redemptive forgiveness, Menahem is welcomed by Judeo-Christians to retake the ministry of the sicarii within the great and holy alliance. By his purifying gesture, Menahem shakes the imperial cult. This affront, made to the man of lies, will be avenged by the hand of the Sadducees who organized the assassination of Menahem on the southern slope of the Temple Mount.

Believers wept once again over the injustice that plagues the martyrs. The romans and their allies once again thought they had put down the revolt. But the good people of Jerusalem were united with their land to support the insurgents in their revolution.

Supporters came from Galilee and Judea to bolster the revolt. Strong and unexpected support came from the Samaritans who came to join the grand alliance. Powerful allies came from the Arab kingdoms and the ancient Partho-Armenian Empire to help the good people of Jerusalem defend themselves.

Gathered on the Temple Mount, the allies laid down their arms and vowed to defend the Temple in Jerusalem. For nearly 4 years, believers were finally able to reclaim the temple. New high priests were appointed and the worship officiated was that of the Judeo-Christians, that is to say as James-the-Just had defined it in his Nazirite compromise: "We have decided not to impose other charges than these which are indispensable. We abstain from meat immolated to idols, from blood, from strangled flesh and from illegitimate unions. »

The capture of Jerusalem and the battles wich occured in the country during the first war of the Jews against the romans are recounted at length by Flavius Josephus in his book The Jewish War. Flavius Josephus was also present throughout the events. During these events, he behaves like a double agent and his role in the war is cloudy... At the end of the Jewish War, he joins the romans he had previously betrayed and to flatter the new strongman of the roman empire, he convinces him to write a book, in the style of the Gallic Wars, that is to say to the glory of the military campaign of the future emperor.

In this book, the roman historian hides behind many lies the truth and somewhere well took him, because without it we would have no testimony of his events. Finally, the romans decided to attack the city of Peace after the burial of Nero in the august mausoleum of the man of lies. Vespasian thus undertook the siege of the holy city which refused to surrender. Jews, Judeo-Christians, Samaritans, Arabs and Armenians stand together and stand united against the oppressor. They talk among themselves about going all the way, about dying to defend the Kingdom. They are convinced in their fight, they will not move! They will stand worthy in the face of liars and strong in the face of death. No, they will not submit!

Vespasian understands the message and begins like Nero to taste the fire. Slowly and methodically, Vespasian and his sons bombard with the catapults and when they break through, they set the city ablaze. With oil and dead wood, they burn the city, they tear open the houses and raze the glory of Jerusalem. Those who refuse slavery are put to death and combatants are killed in battle. Ironically, when the Sadducees were finally presented before their master, he executed them all to the last, thus ending the line of Sadducean priests. Vespasian pretended that the priests had to die with their temple.

News of the fall of Jerusalem was greeted by worshipers of the imperial cult as a great victory. After his triumph in Rome, his legend which wants to be noble and victorious will be nourished by Flavius Josephus who will even go so far as to write that an Essene prophecy had announced the destruction of the temple and that from this event would emerge the new master of the universe: Caesar Vespasian. In truth, the only prophecy in the Book that speaks of this event is the Word of Jesus which was prophesied by Saint Stephen and fulfilled by Menahem: "I will tear down this house and no one can rebuild it. »

"O master Jesus, I am not ashamed to say it, from that time you are the only one who still deserves to be called today by 2 billion human beings: son of God. Your ashes do not rest in an august mausoleum, but your soul lives in the hearts of Christian churches. Through the ages we have heard your message. We come today to lay down our weapons and knock on the doors of the Kingdom, so that Peace reigns on Earth. We are the people of the Book: ahl al-Kitab »

Alleged Bust of Flavius Josephus

Comments from the Word of Jesus

When the reader reads for the first time the collection of the words of Jesus, he looks for the meaning and this search for meaning is at the heart of the teaching of Jesus: to learn to seek in order to find.

I have been studying this book for many years and to participate in a good understanding, I have offered to comment on it. This very rewarding exercise allowed me to make great strides in understanding it and subsequently allowed me to write a historical biography of Jesus as well as the Apostolic Age.

The commentaries are presented according to the order of writing carried out by Thomas and they contain in conferred under acronyms, the places in the Book where the themes or the phraseologies that Jesus uses in this logion are found.

Thank you for appreciating the simplicity of my comments and I wish you a pleasant study.

Here are the hidden words that the living Jesus said that were handwritten by him, Jude named Thomas, the Twin.

1. Jesus says:

"He who understands the meaning of these words will not taste death. »

see JN 8, MT 13, JN 5, PR 3

If we refer to the Dead Sea Scrolls, which tell us about how the Jewish communities lived in the first century in the countryside surrounding Jerusalem, we understand that the culture that prevailed at that time used to cultivate the secret. Thus, Jews and Judeo-Christians did not name things directly, but on the contrary implied truths through well-chosen images.

From this period comes the use of symbols in the Christian tradition. By a symbol the first Christians actually hid a message. Historians often take the example of the name of Kittim which is used in this literature and which in fact designates the romans.

The name Kittim is used in the Old Testament (Maccabees, Book of Daniel) to refer to the invading armies of Alexander the Great. This name comes, according to Flavius Josephus, from the ancient name of Cyprus, Kytion.

COMMENTS

2. Jesus says:

"Let him who seeks cease seeking until he finds. When he finds, he will be tried. After being tested, he will admire and he will reign over all. »

see JS 1

This logion acts as an introduction to the reader of what he is going to be led to in life. As if it were a reading guide for the following logions.

The search for knowledge is a quest of which Jesus summarizes here the main stages.

Inspired by this logion, James-the-Just wrote in his epistle:

"Blessed is the man who will endure the test! Having become a tried man, he will receive the crown of life that God has promised to those who love him. »

3. Jesus says:

"If those who guide you say to you:
'Behold, the Kingdom is in heaven!'
- Then the birds of the sky will be there before you.
If they say to you: 'He is in the sea!'
— Then the fish will be there before you.

But the Kingdom is inside of you
and it is outside of you. When you know yourselves,
then they will recognize you, and you will realize that
you are sons of the living Father.

But if you don't know each other,
then you will be in poverty, you are poor. »

see MT 24, MK 13, LK 17, DT 30, RM 10

People often look outward for what they could find without help from anyone on the inside.

Jesus speaks of those who seek the Kingdom of God and wonder where it is. Jesus explains that the doors of the Kingdom are within oneself and that from knowing oneself comes the ultimate knowledge which leads to recognition.

4. Jesus says:

"The old man at the twilight of his life will not hesitate to question the child of seven days about the place of Life, and he will live!
For there are many first who will become last.
They will return to oneness. »

see MK 10, MT 19, LK 13, JN 17

Some wonder all their lives, others naively ask the youngest. They are the first to ask the question and yet they will be the last to know when they will return to oneness.

Jesus in this logion speaks in a parable of an old man who at the twilight of his life asks a child of seven days where life is.

To explain the images used in this logion, it should be known that according to the Jewish priestly tradition, circumcision takes place on the child on the eighth day of his life (Leviticus 12). The child of seven days is therefore still immaculate from its origin.

It represents in this speech an ideal of purity which has not yet been touched by the knife. It also approaches by this means the subject of circumcision and the Christian reflections which will result from it.

5. Jesus says:

"Know what is before your face,
and what is hidden from you will be revealed to you.
There is nothing hidden
which is sure to be revealed! »

see MT 4, MT 10, LK 8, LK 12

Like many of these logions, this verb always expresses its freshness. The wisdom of its message which expresses a universal truth guides men and women to understand how life works.

By recognizing others at their fair value, the sage sees what is hidden. For he who hides, he is left with the turpitude of knowing that there is nothing hidden that will not fail to be revealed to men or to God.

6.

His disciples questioned him and asked him:
"Do you want us to fast?
How should we pray?
Should we give alms?
Should we abstain from certain foods?

Jesus replied:

- Do not tell a lie, and what is loathsome, do not do it!
Everything is visible in the face of the sky.

There is nothing that is hidden that will not be
discovered. There is nothing covered that will not be
revealed..."

see MT 6, LK 6, RM 7, 2 COR 5, EP 4, COL 3, JS 3, GA 4

The question of the disciples concerns the four classic elements of religious asceticism: fasting, prayer, almsgiving and the choice of food. The disciples ask Jesus what his opinion is on the subject. In his answer, Jesus sends the disciples back to their own reflections which define the nature of Good and Evil. Instead of being interested in the how, Jesus answers to be interested in the why.

Through this journey, the disciple will thus be able to discover what is hidden and reveal the truth. Through the guiding principle, "No lies and nothing loathsome," Jesus teaches his followers to behave like adults rather than like children who expect a normative answer about what is and isn't right to do.

7. Jesus says:

"Well-guided is the lion that man will eat,
the lion became a man.
Wretched is the man whom the lion will eat,
the lion will become like man. »

see 1P5

The meaning of this logion is surely one of the most difficult to penetrate. Its mystery is so thick that this is surely the reason why we find almost nowhere mention of this word in Christian texts. The only reference found in the New Testament literature is in the letters of Peter and as you will see below the reference is very light.

1st letter of Peter, part 5, verse 8:

"Be sober, watch. Your adversary, the devil, prowls around like a roaring lion, seeking whom he will devour. »

Knowing this, it is therefore up to you to know if in the duality of things, you want to be devoured by the lion or if you want to devour the lion...

According to the message of Jesus, this is highly determining, because it will define you as well-guided or wretched..."

8. Jesus says:

"The wise man is like a fisherman who throws a net into the sea. He comes up from the sea full of little fish.

*In the middle of these little fish,
he finds a large and excellent fish.*

*He throws the small fish back into the sea and
chooses the biggest without hesitation.*

Let him who has ears to hear hear! »

see MT 13, LK 5, JN 25, MT 8, LK 4, RM 3

The first Christians who lived persecuted by the roman empire had developed the symbol of the fish as a rallying sign. The origin of this symbol can be found in this logion as well as in the canonical gospels.

The hidden meaning of this parable is quite simple if we reverse the word God in place of the fish. This logion then becomes through the parable, a justification of monotheism in the face of polytheisms.

However, the message of Jesus retains such universal depth that it also works, if we invert the word fish with the words of: saviour, happiness, value, knowledge, etc.

Ichthys or ichthus means fish in Greek (ΙΧΘΥΣ or ΙΧΘΥC). The Christian fish is made up of two intersecting arcs, with the ends on the right side extending beyond the meeting point to resemble the profile of the fish. The early Christians adopted it as a secret symbol. It was a sign of recognition that allowed people to recognize themselves without being spotted by the roman authorities.

ΙΧΘΥΣ (ichthus) is an acronym meaning "Iēsous Christos Theou Yios Sōtēr (Ἰησοῦς Χριστός, Θεοῦ Υἱός y'jos, Σωτήρ) that is to say: "Jesus Christ, Son of God, Savior".

9. Jesus says:

"Behold, the sower came out
hand full of seeds to sow.
Some fell on the road,
the birds came and picked them.

Some fell on the rock.
They have not found where to sink their roots nor
have they managed to rise to the sky.

Others have fallen among the thorns
who choked them and the worm ate them.
Others finally fell on the good ground,
these brought forth an excellent fruit.
They gave sixty per measure.
They gave up to one hundred and twenty per
measure. »

see MT 13, MK 4, LK 8, JN 12, 2 COR 9

In this parable of the sower, who sows the ground? Who is the Sower? Who does He represent?

And what are the seeds he sows if not also food?

Mark in his canonical gospel sees in this term seed, the divine word. A word of wisdom which will multiply the gains and give sixty per measure or even one hundred and twenty per measure.

10. Jesus says:

"I have cast a fire on the world, and here I am watching over it until it spreads. »

see LK 12

The fact that this word of Jesus is taken up only by Luke accredits the theory that the said Gospel of Thomas was used independently by the authors of the Gospels of Matthew, Mark, Luke and John. It also accredits the thesis that this text was at the origin.

When Luke takes up this Word, he interprets and writes:

"I have come to throw a fire on the earth, and what have I to desire if it is already lit? There is a baptism with which I must be baptized, and how long I long for it to be accomplished…"

In writing this, Luke picks up the theme of the baptism of Jesus by the fire of the saintly spirit. Fire representing heat and light.

This use of the parable of Light and its representation by fire is typical of Christian teaching. We find, moreover, its representation in the halos of Christian saints. Because as it is said in the canonical gospels, John the Baptist baptized with the purity of water while Jesus baptized with the fire of the saintly spirit.

11. Jesus says:

"This sky will pass away, and he who is above it will
pass away. The dead have no life,
the living have no death.

Today you eat dead things and make living ones.

When you're in the light,
what will you do on that day?
You were in oneness then you became two, became
two, what will you do? »

We do not clearly find this logion in the New Testament and this confirms that the Gospel of Thomas was not entirely taken up. The phraseology, "this heaven will pass away," is used extensively, but it is unclear whether these terms represent typical Jesus phraseology or simply common wording.

The first part of the logion vaguely recalls the theme of the impermanence of all things and in the second part of the logion, Jesus speaks again of one of his favorite themes and explains to the disciples that division is only a stage leading to Unity.

12. The disciples said to Jesus:

"We know you will leave us. Who will be great above us?

Jesus answers them

- At the point where you will be, you will go to James the Just, it is for him that the earth and the sky were created. »

These twelveth logion like so many others is indicative of the authenticity of this collection of words. Because it also demonstrates the importance attached by the early Christians to the word that had been spoken.

Historians are confirming this sayings because it is James the Just who is mentioned as the first bishop of Jerusalem in all the ecclesiastical lists, although, he is never named first in the nomenclatures of the disciples. The reason, why James was named as first bishop or Kingdom's heir is simply found in this logion.

For the most skeptical, the historical reality of the existence of James-the-Just is hardly in doubt. His execution is mentioned in a passage from the Jewish Antiquities of Flavius Josephus and the ossuary in which his bones laid was found in Israel in 2002.

13. Jesus said to his disciples:

"Compare me. Tell me who I am like. »

Simon Peter says:
"You are like a righteous angel. »

Matthew says:
"You are like a wise and philosophical man. »

Thomas said to him:
"Master, who are you like...?"
My mouth can't grasp it. »

Jesus replied:
"I am not your master, because you have been
drinking. You have satiated yourselves at the gushing
spring of which I have taken the measure..."

Then he grabbed Thomas and they pulled away.
Then he said three words to him.
When Thomas returned to his companions,

They asked him:
"What did Jesus tell you? »

Thomas answered them, "If I said one word to you
that he said to me, you would pick up stones and
stone me. A fire will come out of it and you will burn!"

see MT 16, MK 8, LK 9, JN 10

"Who do you think I am? ". The question is asked in the 4 canonical gospels as in the said Gospel of Thomas.

14. Jesus says to them:

"When you fast, you will beget sin for yourselves. When you pray, they will condemn you. When you give alms, you will do harm to your spirits...

When you go into a country and walk through the countryside, if they welcome you, eat what they put before you.

And those who are sick in those places, heal them! For what goes into your mouth will not defile you, but what comes out of your mouth will defile you! »

see MT 10, LK 10, MK 7

In this logion, Jesus questions the meaning of religious regulations and questions the meaning of his habits and customs, because he fears that the fruits of his activities may be bad.

Indeed, fasting is a deprivation which, badly guided, can lead to weakening the body, if it is done on a fragile person, it can even become dangerous. Likewise, those who see you praying may think you have a lot to be forgiven for. If you give alms without a genuine reason, you risk poisoning your mind with futile considerations.

Through his message, Jesus says that what heals people's hearts are genuine good deeds.

15. *Jesus says:*

"When you see him who was not begotten of the female, prostrate yourself face down and adore him, for he is your Father! »

see MT 26, JOS 5, NB 20, AP 7, NE 8, MT 17: 6

This word of Jesus, as well as other references from the Old Testament (or Tanakh), are generally used by Muslims to justify the face down position performed during Muslim prayer.

In general, many terms from the verb of Jesus are found abundantly in the Koran and in the case of this logion, it is the term defining God as the one who has not been begotten. The reason for this fact recognized by Muslim historians and theologians comes from the influence of Judeo-Christianity which is the foundation of the Muslim religion.

If we look for a hidden meaning in this logion, it could be that of a veiled criticism of men and women who bow down to the rich and powerful. These are begotten of woman and do not deserve such outpourings of adoration and submission. Because from a theological point of view worship or submission must be directed towards God, so as not to have idolatrous morals.

16. Jesus says:

*"**Certainly men think that I have come to sow peace in the world. But they do not know that I have come to throw away the means of division:***

fire, sword and war.

If indeed there are five in a house, they will be three against two and two against three, the father against the son and the sons against the fathers. They will rise united as one. »

see MT 10, LK 12

This logion is one of the most mysterious in the collection of Jesus' words. To be honest with you, I can't tell you for sure what it means. This commentary is therefore intended to be more exploratory than explanatory.

In this logion, we glimpse the theme of the final battle, which represents the last test that will leads to unity. Then division is seen as just a part of the process who leads to Unity (see Logion 11).

In the symbol of fire, I think we must see the teaching of Jesus. In the symbol of the sword, I think we should see the ardor of the Sicarii. In the symbol of war, in my opinion, we must see the theme found in the literature of the Dead Sea Scrolls, which is that of the final battle between the sons of Light and the sons of Darkness.

The 5 members of the house could be on one side those who represent the fathers, that is to say the Sadducees and the Pharisees. The three sons could be: the Essenes, the Sicarii and the Nazirs.

Finally, if we refer to the Dead Sea Scrolls and the Jewish Antiquities of Flavius Josephus, Jewish society in the 1st century AD was an extremely divided society and there was a significant division that separated people urban and rural, the riches and the ascetics, the materialistics and the spirituals, the realists and the mystics, the foreign immigrants and the native locals, the Jews and the Christians...

17. Jesus says:

"I will give you what no eye has seen.
I will give you what ears have never heard.
I will give you what no hand has ever touched.
I'll give you what never occured to you. »

see 1CO2

As you may have noticed, this logion was only taken up by Paul in his epistle to the Corinthians (Christians who lived in Greece in the Peloponnese). The fact that Paul alone quotes this logion, combined with the fact that he quotes it clearly and in its entirety, proves historically by literary means that the Word of Jesus contained in the Gospel of Thomas precedes the writing of Paul's epistles.

To go further, we can also ask ourselves the reasons that led him to take over this particular logion. For Paul generally abstains from quoting the words of Jesus contained in the Gospels.

If we follow the traditional chronological order, Paul knew that this logion had not been taken up in the Gospel of Matthew or Mark. So he knew that by using this logion, he would make a masterstroke. On the one hand, he would subtly demonstrate that the Word of Jesus preceded the Gospels and on the other hand, he would silence his detractors who reproached him for not taking up the Word of Jesus. The icing on the cake, he takes up a stylistic figure of Jesus that requires no comment... In three words: hats off, Maestro.

18. The disciples said to Jesus:

"Tell us, how will our end come?

Jesus replies:

**Have you ever unveiled the beginning,
so that you wonder about the end?**

Where the beginning is, there will be our end.

Well-guided is he who will stand in the beginning, he will know the end from then on and he will not taste death. »

What nostalgia, to read this marvelous logion and to see that the classical authors have not taken it up. It is true that the successive authors had to make choices and that he could not take everything back anyway, because the content is too rich and too deep.

In this typical verb of Jesus, we can deduce that these words come from one and the same person, because we find the style of response that Jesus gave when one asked him a question. Jesus thus answered with a question that suggests the answer.

Finally, to contradict myself with the first paragraph, I invite the reader to ask themselves, if despite everything, the themes of this logion do not transpire somewhere in the New Testament? A line of thought should be sought in John's final work.

***Symbol combining the
Chrism and the alpha and omega***

The chrism is signified by the two Greek letters Khi and Rho (XP) which together signify Christ.

ALPHA & OMEGA are signified by the two Greek letters alpha (A) and omega (Ω) which signify the beginning and the end of the Greek alphabet and by extrapolation the Whole.

19. *Jesus says:*

**"*Well-guided is he who was before he became!*
If you become my disciples and listen to my words,
*these will serve you like stones.***

**There are five trees in Paradise which change neither
summer nor winter. Their leaves do not fall.**

Whoever knows them will not taste death! »*

see AP 2, GN 2

The use of imagery (stones) is one of the striking styles in the Word of Jesus. This means is called among Christians: Parable.

During the study of this logion, I went to look in the Book of Enoch, because in this book, the subject of the trees of Paradise is present and also because all the historical clues let us think that his study was still followed by Essenes during the 1st century AD.

In the book of Enoch, we find scattered between chapters 25 and 32 the mentions of several trees: there is the marvelous tree, whose fruits provide immortality, and which will be given to the justs and the chosens. There is the permanent tree whose branches grow even when cut. The tree of judgment which exhales a sweet odor of incense and myrrh, a beautiful fragrant tree of resin from mastic tree and a tree of wisdom whose fruit those who eat it possess great wisdom and of which Adam and Eve tasted.

20. The disciples said to Jesus:

"Tell us: what does the Kingdom of Heaven look like?

He answered them:

"The Kingdom of Heaven is like a mustard seed, that is, the smallest of all seeds.

When it falls on the plowed ground, it produces a large stem which becomes a shelter for birds. »

see MT 13, MK 4, LK 13

It is because Jesus speaks of the Kingdom of Heaven that the disciples ask him what it looks like. Instead of a description of the place, Jesus gives them a parable of what it looks alike: with almost nothing, it gives a lot.

<u>Note on the disciples:</u> According to Luke 10, there were 70 disciples. Christian tradition refers to them as the seventy disciples. Jesus then dispatched them in groups of two to different regions to announce the coming of the Kingdom. In some versions of the Bible, the number of disciples is 72. The same is true in several texts of Eastern Christianity. Presumably each of the 12 apostles was responsible for discipleship. Thus, there would then be 12 groups of 6 disciples, each group having at its head a formative apostle. These twelve groups of evangelical formation would therefore have been formed each of seven members for a total of 84, it means 72 disciples plus the 12 apostles.

The Twelve called "apostles" in the Gospel according to Luke (Lk 6,13), represent those who are sent on mission (etymology of the word apostle), they are accompanied by their pupils (disciples), but above all they remain disciples of Jesus.

Their list of names is given four times in the New Testament: the twelve apostles are: Peter, Andrew, James the great (the brother of John), John, Philippe, Bartholomew, Thomas, Matthew, James the less (James-the-Just), Jude-the-Zélot, Simon-the-Zélot and Judas the Iscariot-Sicarii (replaced by Matthias).

Paul of Tarsus is considered the thirteenth apostle, he is qualified as the apostle of the gentiles (i.e. of the uncircumcised). He is also often referred to as the fifth evangelist (for the place of his letters in the New Testament).

The Twelve Apostles are chosen by Jesus Christ to be, apart from their evangelizing mission, a symbol for the people of Israel: their number of twelve evokes the twelve tribes of Israel (source Wikipedia).

Moreover, the numbers 12 and 70 are a reminder of the Old Testament and of the children of Jacob, named Israel, this name means according to Flavius Josephus, the one who fights with God. Jacob had 12 children who are at the base of the 12 tribes of Israel, when with his grandchildren they come to join Joseph in Egypt, he comes accompanied by his grandchildren, the total number excluding Jacob is 70... Thus, we understand that, like Jacob, Jesus is the patriarch of a new people.

21. Mary Magdalene asked Jesus:

"To whom are your disciples like? »

He replies:

*"They are like little children who have entered a field
that does not belong to them.
When the owners of the field come,
they say :*

"Leave our field! »

*So, like children, they take off their clothes, leave the
field and return it.*

That's why I say:

*"If the householder knows the thief is coming.
He will watch before he arrives, and he will not let
him dig an entrance into the house of his kingdom in
order to take away his wealth.*

*You too ! Be vigilant in this world. Gird your loins
with great energy, so that the brigands do not find a
way to reach you, because the profit you watch, they
will find it!*

So be aware and prepared!

*For when the fruit is ripe,
he comes with his sickle to pick it...*

Let him who has ears to hear hear! »

see MT 24, MK 13, LK 12, MK 4, AP 16: 15

This logion testifies to the place of Mary Magdalene among the disciples, her status is confirmed by the fact that she is specifically named. It also demonstrates that Jesus spoke freely to women. The fact that he caters to women as well as men has a strong meaning for this period, because the conservative culture of the Essenes and Jews of the 1st century AD had a misogynistic image of the women they accused of being responsible as much as Eve, for the expulsion of humans from the Garden of Eden...

To develop the meaning of this logion, many interpreters correctly see the field in which the disciples go as the pictorial field of knowledge.

Behind the image of the master of the house, the reader is entitled to wonder if he is just not simply Jesus? Because Jesus teaches the disciples, as adults teach little children. His speech on the subjects of vigilance and preparation testifies to great maturity.

Finally, note the use of the famous phraseology of Jesus:

"Whoever has ears to hear, hear! »

22. Jesus saw little ones suckling
and he said to his disciples:

"These little ones who suckle are like those who enter
the Kingdom.

The disciples asked him, "If we are small (less), will
we enter the Kingdom?"

Jesus answered them:

"When you make one with two,
that you will make the inside like the outside and the
outside like the inside.

When you're up and down
and the bottom as the top,
When you unite the masculine and the feminine. So
that what is not masculine becomes man. So that
what is not feminine becomes woman.

When you have eyes in your eyes, a hand in your
hand, a foot in your foot, and an image in your image.

That's when you'll get in! »

see MT 18, MK 9, LK 9, JN 17

In my opinion, in this logion, Jesus addresses a fundamental theme of his doctrine, which is to achieve Unity through Fullness. This state where one link with a good understanding, what seems contrary. This higher state of consciousness which leads to Harmony and Clairvoyance.

COMMENTS

23. Jesus said:

"I will choose you, one from a thousand and two from ten thousand and they will rise as one!" »

see MT 22, 14

In this work, I first privilege the literary proofs which confirm by the classical authors that the Word of Jesus, contained in the Angile, precedes the writing of the canonical Gospels (Evangile).

According to the Church Fathers Irenaeus of Lyon and Epiphanius of Salamis, this word was widely used by the Basilidian Gnostics as justification for an elitist doctrine of knowledge (gnosis means knowledge in ancient Greek).

These affirmations of the fathers of the Church thus prove that by this logion, the Word of Jesus is at the origin of the right and the wrong interpretation.

Finally, to return to the meaning of this logion, this word recalls the Old Testament and the military doctrine that Jethro gave to Moses: he encouraged him to organize his army with leaders at the head of 10,000, 1,000, 500, 100 and 50 soldiers.

In my interpretation of the political balance of power in the Jewish society of the 1st century, I think that this word concerns the organization of the ministry of Jesus (Jesus + James the Just = 10,000, the ministers minimum 1000).

24. His disciples said to him:

"Instruct us where you are, for we must seek it! »

He says to them:
"Let him who has ears to hear, hear!

If a light exists within a man of light, then that light illuminates the world. If it does not become light, what darkness! »

see MT 6, 23, LK 11, 33-36, JN 1, 4-11

It is with these kinds of requests that the master recognizes good disciples. Those who want to know and who are in spontanuous search of knowledge are always in the end the good disciples.

Touched by the request of his disciples who ask to free themselves, Jesus gives them a final answer. Whoever wants to free himself and become an adult must learn to seek by himself the light that guides his path. Better to follow the Light that illuminates the world than to sink into darkness...

25. Jesus said:

**"Love your brother as your soul,
watch over him as over the apple of your eye. »**

see LV 19, MT 5, MK 12, RM 13, GA 5, JS 2, 1 JN 2, etc.

No one doubt about the authenticity of this saying.

60 generations have since passed and yet John's commentary in his first epistle remains as relevant as ever. In the dark times we live in, it enlightens judgment:

"Whoever claims to be in the light while hating his brother is still in darkness.

He who loves his brother dwells in the light and there is no occasion for him to fall.

But he who hates his brother is in darkness, he walks in darkness, he does not know where he is going, because darkness has blinded his eyes. »

26. Jesus says:

*"The speck that is in your brother's eye, you see it.
But the beam that is in your eye, you do not see it!*

*When you have taken out the beam that is in your eye,
then you will see how to remove the speck from your
brother's eye. »*

see MT 7, LK 6

Logions 25 and 26 are among the most famous words of Jesus and the use of this logion has even passed into common parlance. The image of this message is so common that many are unaware of its Christian origin.

If this message and this parable could so easily fit into the most famous proverbs, it is because Jesus easily explains a difficult message. In a few well-chosen words, he makes us understand so much and even after reflection, there is always something to understand, because behind images people will seek to replace them with words, because that is the meaning of this riddle. And the word of Jesus is so rich that it suggests the answer to adopt in his life.

In the Words of Jesus, we find many of what I call universal truths. It means immutable wisdom that transcends the cultures of this world and that will remain, through the ages, always true.

IN HOC SIGNO VINCES

In hoc signo vinces is a Latin phrase translated from ancient Greek "ἐν τούτῳ νίκα", which can be translated as: "By this sign, you will conquer". Lactantius (c. 250 - c. 325) reports that Constantine I had a vision of the chrism (☧) in the sky shortly before the Battle of the Milvian Bridge, which took place in 312.

Church historian Eusebius of Caesarea indicates that Constantine was marching with his army when he looked at the sun and saw a cross of light within, with the Greek inscription (ἐν) τούτῳ νίκα. Constantine did not at first understand the meaning of this apparition, but the following night he had a dream in which Christ explained to him that he had to use the sign of the cross against his enemies. According to the legend, the symbol will be used and this will allow Constantine to win the battle of the Milvian Bridge despite being outnumbered. Constantine I will then convert to Christianity and become the first Christian Roman emperor. His conversion will greatly promote the growth of Christianity. Constantine I is recognized by the Orthodox Greeks as a saint as well as his mother who will be at the origin of the construction of the Holy Sepulcher in Jerusalem.

27. Jesus says:

"If you don't fast from this world then you won't find the Kingdom. If you don't make the Sabbath, the Sabbath, you won't see the Father. »

see MT 5, LK 12, JN 3

Fasting from this world is one of the peculiarities of the lifestyle of ascetics. Asceticism is a voluntary discipline of body and mind seeking to strive for perfection. Asceticism as a moral exercise is found in all religions, but its use is not limited to these.

This logion bears witness to the ascetic views of Jesus. These ascetic customs were also shared by John the Baptist and by the nazirs. This logion and its way of thinking are still found today in the lives of Christian monks who in their monasteries force themselves in their acts to fast from this world, to find the Kingdom.

« If you don't make the Sabbath, the Sabbath, that you will see the Father. » In this formulation, we distinguish an idea that Jesus has already addressed in Logion 22. That is to say, that of defining a righteous being. Jesus then said that to be just you must have: eyes in your eyes, a hand in your hand, a foot in your foot and an image in your image. By these preceding images, one should understand right vision, right action, right means and right self-awareness. In this logion, Jesus adds that we must also have a just respect for the laws of Moses (tradition).

28. Jesus says:

"I stood in the midst of the world and in the flesh I manifested myself to them. I found them all drunk and I found none thirsty.

My soul is grieved over the children of men. Because they are blind in their heart and do not see why they came into the world. Empty, they came into the world, without anything, they will leave it...

Someone come and straighten them up, because here they are staggering! When they have slept off their wine, they will repent of it. »

<u>No comment.</u>

29. Jesus says:

"If the flesh came into existence through the spirit, that is wonderful. But if the spirit came into existence through the body, it is a marvelous marvel.

I'm rather surprised by this:

How was this great wealth placed in this poverty? »

Jesus addresses in this logion an existential debate on the origin of life. Which came first, is it the body or the mind? This debate, which is said to be endless, is at the heart of the chicken-and-egg paradox. This famous paradox begins with the following question: which came first: the chicken or the egg? If you are told "It's the egg", you ask "Who laid this egg?" ". If you are told "It's the hen", you ask "But this hen is hatching from an egg, isn't it? ".

The paradox comes from the fact that no answer seems satisfactory. Jesus understood this well, so he answers in a satisfactory way, whether the body or the spirit appeared first, in either case, it is wonderful. After having, in a few words, closed this debate, Jesus asks his disciples a question which leads the listener to ask another unanswered question… In all likelihood with his teaching, great wealth is spiritual while poverty is his during body.

30. Jesus says:

"Where there are three gods, they are gods. Where there are two or one, I am with Him! »

This logion is quite clear when one understands the monotheistic teaching of Jesus' message. Without this key to understanding, we remain perplexed by this word that mixes polytheism, dualism and monotheism.

"Where there are three gods, they are gods". In this polytheistic case, Jesus is not with them. In case there are two. One representing the supreme being, the other representing an inferior and contrary being, i.e. the false God, the usurper, the stranger, Satan. In this context, Jesus is with the Eternal who represents one.

31. Jesus says:

"No one is a prophet in his village. No one is the doctor of his relatives. »

see MT 13, LK 4, JN 4, MK 6

Like logion 26, this word has passed into everyday French language. In this logion Jesus expresses a very human paradox. The human needs to obtain the recognition of others and he needs to heal his loved ones of their possible ailments. Yet as Jesus puts it, there is nothing more difficult and sometimes it is even impossible to achieve.

So, if you wish to be someone, don't do it to obtain recognition from others or to obtain a rewarding power, just simply do it for yourself, for your personal fulfillment in the present life and in the future life. Thus, you will get what you are looking for.

32. Jesus says:

"A stronghold built on a high hill. Nothing can bring it down, nothing can hide it. »

see MT 5, EP 6

When I read this logion, I cannot stop seeing in this stronghold built on a high hill, the image of the fortress of Masada. This ancient fortification placed on a limestone rock overlooking the Dead Sea and which is the symbol of an entire people.

Jesus calls the listener in this parable to stand like a fortified city: high above others, solid, unique, admirable, beyond the shadow of a doubt.

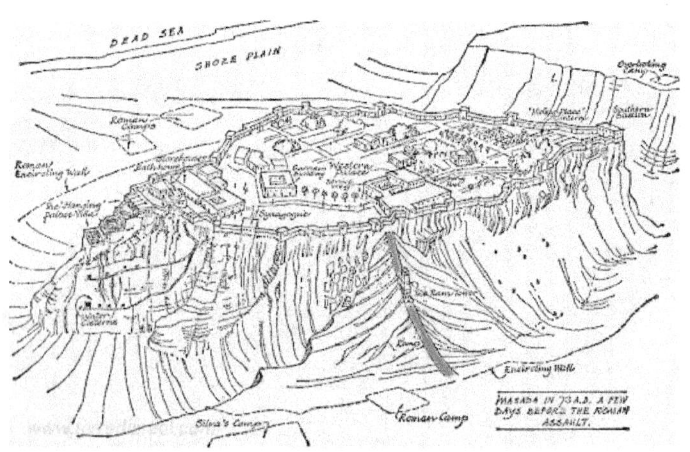

33. Jesus says:

*"What you will hear with your ears,
teach it to others and shout it from the rooftops!*

*No one lights a lamp to put it under a bushel, nor
does one put the lamp in a hidden place. Rather, it is
placed on the candelabrum so that all who enter and
leave see its light. »*

see MT 5, LK 11, JN 4, MK 4

The clearest logions are those that are most repeated in the canonical gospels. Their meanings are simple to understand and are unanimous in the canonical gospels. Thus this word of Jesus is also found in each of the 4 canonical gospels.

9 branch Ménorah

COMMENTS

34. Jesus says:

***"If a blind man leads another blind man,
both will fall into a pit. »***

see MT 15, LK 6, JN 4, RM 2

In this logion, Jesus uses the parable of the blind man and the blind driver. One can rightly ask who Jesus designates behind the names of the blind and who are the blind leaders?

Maybe the answer is in the following logion…

35. Jesus says:

"It is not possible for anyone to take the house of a strong man by force without first binding his hands, only then can he plunder his house. »

see MT 12, LK 11, MK 3

Wouldn't this word of Jesus be a premonition of events to come? When Jesus came to the temple in Jerusalem and set out to drive the merchants and the saducees sacrifiers out of the temple, he did this by pulling together ropes and cracking them like a whip (John 2).

Giambattista Tiepolo, 1730

36. Jesus said:

"Do not worry from evening to morning or from morning to evening, what clothes you will wear. »

see MT 6, LC 12

The meaning of this word confirms the ascetic teachings of Jesus, because he advocates detachment and the renunciation of the pleasures of the senses. The ascetic view correctly argues that one cannot achieve a permanent state of satisfaction by endlessly pursuing one's desires. This reasoning is confirmed in the bitter observation that one desire always replaces another desire.

The ascetics profess that it is in spiritual fulfillment that the human being is able to obtain the lasting satisfaction from his human condition.

Finally, this logion is to be compared with the historical descriptions made by Flavius Josephus of the uniforms worn by the Essenes.

37. His disciples asked him:

***"When will you manifest yourself to us?
When will we see you? »***

Jesus replies:

***"When you undress shamelessly and trample your
clothes like little children do. Then you will see the
Son of the Living One and you will no longer be
afraid. »***

The image of children trampling on their clothes has already been used previously in Logion 21. This image of nudity which frees itself from its clothing shackles to return to nature, is an image which is inspired by the story of Adam and Eve in Genesis:

"The woman saw that the tree was good to eat and pleasant to the sight, that it was precious for opening up the intelligence. She took of its fruit and ate it. She also gave it to her husband, who was with her, and he ate it. The eyes of both were opened, they knew that they were naked, and having sewn fig leaves, they made themselves belts. »

38. Jesus says:

"Many times have you longed to hear the words I speak to you. And, there is no one else you will be able to hear them from. The days will come when you will look for me and will not find me.

see JN 7, LK 10, MT 13

This logion is a rhetorical figure of speech called antithesis. When we study the eloquence of Jesus, we realize that he had a very complete oral style. There are similes, metaphors and analogies. There are parables, personifications and allegories. There are innuendoes, ellipses and irony.

When we add to this a noble feeling of humanity, a moral depth and an unshakable conviction, we understand that we have in front of us an exceptional young man.

39. Jesus says:

"The Pharisees and the scribes took the keys of knowledge and hid them. They did not dare to open the door and they did not let others enter.

But you, know how cunning is the serpent and stay pure like the dove. »

see LK 11, MT 23, MT 10

In the Jewish religion, the Pharisees are looked upon with respect. Because, historically, they are the ones who, at the end of the great revolt, revived, in the year 73, the Jewish religion after its defeat by the roman Empire. They are considered to be those who took the priesthood back into their own hands and solved the problems caused by the destruction of the temple.

In the Christian religion, on the contrary, the Pharisees are regarded with contempt because of the teaching of Jesus, who in his words reproaches them for deducing by their interpretations of false laws and especially for hiding the knowledge and the reading of the Book to the greatest number.

Knowing this, it is for the reader to avoid any anachronistic bias that would distort his understanding. This is why it is necessary to take a historical step back with past events and above all not to make today's believers feel guilty because of the alleged errors of their ancestors.

40. Jesus said:

"A vine stock has been planted apart from the Father. And since it is not strong, it will be torn from the root and he will perish…"

see PR 12, JR 2, EZ 19, MT 3, JN 15, COL 2

The parable of the vine is not unique to Jesus, this image is a classic analogy found in many authors. This image and its counterpart : the root, is even used a lot in Indian and Asian cultures. It is surely because the symbolism it conveys is easy to understand that its use is universal.

41. Jesus says:

"Whoever has in his hand, it will be given to him. But he who does not have, even the little he has, it will be taken away. »

see LK 8, MT 13, MK 4

The characteristic of the messengers of Truth is to speak the Truth. It is the essence of their message to find the words to express a human truth that remains universal.

But we must not see in this universal truth: a fatality. For Jesus, in his deeds and his words, showed compassion towards the weak and the helpless. He wanted a life of asceticism and sharing where this earthly truth would be supplanted by a heavenly vision which he called the Kingdom.

I regard the messages of Truth as the light that shines on the horizon of Humanity. I contemplate in the distance this stable, fixed and certain line. It serves me as a reference and thanks to its teaching my spirit rises!

42. Jesus says:

"Come into being as you pass away. »

see JN 13:1, 1 COR 4:11

The majority of French translations of this logion give the meaning to this verb: be passing. This is a good, short and punchy translation.

For those who speak English, you will find below the original English translation which serves as a support for modern translations of this text. The work was done by Michael W. Grondin between 1997 and 2002 and we thank him for it.

Excerpt from his translation

ΠΕΧΕ·ΙC	ΧΕ	·ϢⲰΠⲈ	ⲈⲦⲈⲦⲚ·Ⲣ·ⲠⲀⲢⲀⲄⲈ
*Said-JS42	this:	come-into-being	as-you(pl)-pass-away.

My translation is certainly more literal, but it has the advantage of keeping the Christian theme of rebirth. According to the Acts of the Apostles, when the church in Jerusalem was founded, the first Christians entered the new life by mourning their past life. During this rebirth, some even changed their names. The reader is entitled to wonder if the reason for this behavior is not simply due to the teaching of this logion.

43. His disciples called out to him:

"Who are you ? You, who tell us these things? »

Jesus replies:

"By the things I tell you,
don't you recognize who I am?

You are like some Judeans
who love the tree and hate its fruit,
who love the fruit and hate its tree…"

see LK 6:43-44, JN 8:25

We find in this logion the themes of logion 5:

"Know what is before your face, and what is hidden from you
will be revealed to you. Because, there is nothing hidden that
will not fail to be revealed! »

Learn to recognize the fruit by its tree.
While learning to recognize the tree by its fruit.

One is reflected in the other.
They are united from the beginning to the end.

44. Jesus says:

"Whoever slanders against the father, he will be forgiven. Whoever slanders against the son, he will be forgiven. But he who slanders against the spirit of holiness. This one, neither on earth nor in heaven, will be forgiven. »

see MT 12, MK 3, LK 12

The word spirit of holiness is usually translated in Christian literature as Holy Spirit. If we replace in this logion, the words spirit of holiness by Holy Spirit, we have the appearance of a word of Jesus which prefigures the Christian belief in a divine trinity: the Father, the Son and the Holy Spirit. However, the deep meaning of this verb seems rather to indicate the opposite. Jesus says those who slander the image of the father, or the image of the son will be forgiven while those who slander the image of the holy spirit will not be forgiven… So there is a ranking between these three representations.

In a parallel logion, Jesus says: "In the image of the Father, the image will be hidden by the light. » In this logion the images of the Father and of the son are found hidden by the light of the Holy Spirit… We find several times in the literature of the Old Testament and consequently in the Tanakh, the idea that the ideal essence of God is a spirit of holiness, Isaiah wrote: *"The Spirit of the Lord shall rest upon him: Spirit of wisdom and understanding, Spirit of counsel and strength, Spirit of knowledge and fear of the Lord. »* Isaiah: 11 -2

45. Jesus says:

"We don't harvest grapes from brambles.
Nor are figs picked from the thistles.
This is because they do not produce fruit!

The good man brings good things out of his attic.
The evil man draws from his attic, which is none
other than his evil heart, bad things and from his
mouth come out horrors.

Of the abundance of the spirit,
bad things come out. »

see MT 7, LK 7

<u>No comment.</u>

46. Jesus says:

"From Adam to John the Baptist among those begotten of women there is none greater than John the Baptist.

It is because his vision is right that it is said that his eyes will not be broken!

That's why I say:

Who among you will become small (less), that one will know the Kingdom and he will rise above John the Baptist. »

see MT 11, MT 12, LK 6

First of all, I want to point out to the reader that the part "his view is right" is an addition on my part to help the reader understand the meaning behind this sentence. Without addition the sentence is: "Therefore his eyes will not be broken". The eyes representing the idea of what he sees, i.e. his vision.

To comment on the meaning of this logion, I first find that it testifies to Jesus' admiration for John the Baptist, then I find that it also testifies to the meaning that Jesus gave to greatness. He who will make himself even more humble than the admirable ascetic that John the Baptist was, he will become even greater.

47. Jesus says:

"It is not possible for a man to ride two horses, nor to draw two bows.
It is not possible for a servant to serve two masters, otherwise he would honor one and despise the other!

Never does a man drink old wine and immediately desire to drink new wine.

New wine is not poured into old wineskins lest they burst.

Old wine is not poured into new skins, lest they spoil.

You do not sew an old piece on a new garment, because a tear would occur. »

see MT 6, JN 2, LK 16, MT 9, LK 5, MK 2

In this logion, Jesus affirms these monotheistic beliefs and he advocates the choice to follow the honorable master rather than submit to the despicable master...

He also expresses that his choice is irreversible.

Because :

"New wine is not poured into old wineskins lest they burst. Old wine is not poured into new skins, lest they spoil. You do not sew an old piece on a new garment, because a tear would occur. »

48. *Jesus says:*

**"*If two make peace in a house, when they say to the mountain:*
'Go away!' then it will go away. »**

see MT 17, MK 11, 1 COR 13, LK 17

It is through peace that one can achieve unity. It is through unity that the impossible can be reversed to the possible. All these inequalities that separate us… These forces that seem unshakable to us. Nothing resists the human being when he finds through Peace the means to make Unity.

Often we hear people say that Peace and Unity are unattainable goals, because the differences are so great that they become insurmountable. However, whether on the scale of a lifetime or on the scale of History, we realize that human beings and Humanity tend towards this absolute of Unity and Peace.

As Jesus conceptualizes in this logion, division comes from an existential duality that represents the two extremes of everything: up and down, left and right, heads and tails, light and dark, feminine and masculine, spiritual and bestial, good and evil, vice and virtue, self-interest and common interest, plus and minus, form and substance, etc. and the anti-etc.…

Instead of continually opposing them and seeing them as by nature irreconcilable, you should know that it is always possible to find a framework, that is to say "a house", where you can reconcile them. This framework can take different forms and the easy example of its representation is that of a peace treaty which by convention and the recognition of the two parties defines a peaceful framework where the two parties can evolve together in the future.

This debate does not only exist outside, but takes place primarily inside oneself. This is why it is decisive for its well-being to reconcile in a peaceful setting the multiple divisions that drive us.

Personally, I do not know if without the teaching of the Book descended in the name of God, I could have found the means to make Peace and Unity with the enemy parts that shape my personality. What helped me in my understanding was to understand that although these sensitivities are different, they are in reality all seeking to achieve the same objective or to meet the same need. That is to say that their opposition is in form, because in substance they share the same objective.

49. Jesus says:

"Well-guided are you, the united and the chosen, for you will find the Kingdom.

You came from it and you will return there. »

see JN 8:42

What is interesting in the study of this logion is the use of the word chosen. This term suggests that Jesus was aware of the book of Enoch, because in this book which was still studied in his time the term chosen appears 49 times. In the text of Enoch, this term represents those who will inherit the earth (Chapter V).

What is also interesting in this logion is the use of the term united which is also sometimes translated by monakos (this term will later give the name of monk). This term is specific to the verb of Jesus and its idea is found several times in various forms. In all likelihood with his teaching, this title designates human beings who have succeeded in creating Unity and Peace within themselves, i.e those who caress fullness and wholeness with their finger.

Finally, the last sentence expresses the idea that unity passes through God, because the united are also those who seek to make union with Him. He who makes the union between the beginning and the end.

50. Jesus says:

"If people ask you:
where did you come into existence?

Tell them:
We came from the light, from the place where the
light was born. He appeared in their image.

If you are asked: who are you?

Tell them:
We are his sons and we are the chosen of the living
Father.

Finally, if they ask you what does it mean that the
Father is in you?

Tell them:
It is movement and rest. »

CF. LK 16, JN 12, EP 5, 1 TH 5, 1 JN 1, JN 1

In this logion Jesus performs a monologue in which he makes the questions and the answers. The questions have surely been formulated to him previously and he provides his answers here. The first answer in this logion seems to be a reference to the Book of Genesis. The second answer expresses a word similar to that of the Dead Sea Scrolls, where we find the expression of the sons of Light. Finally, the last sentence, which seems antithetical, expresses the idea that thanks to God, human beings find the means to unite opposites.

51. His disciples asked him:

"When will the day of rest for the dead come? When will the day of the advent of the new world come? »

Jesus answers them:

"What you expect has already happened, and yet you did not recognize it. »

CF. LK 17, JN 5, EP 5, 1 TH 5, 1 JN 1, JN 1

Through his discourse on the immortality of the soul and his discourse on the existence after death of a Place of Rest for the deserving, Jesus brings rest for the dead. By his words and deeds as well as by his ultimate sacrifice, Jesus opens the doors to a new world for believers, whatever their origins.

Jesus teaches these disciples to learn to recognize things and people for what they really are. It means he teaches to become clairvoyant.

Notes :

Although there was no belief in an afterlife with reward or punishment in Judaism before 200 BC. in later Judaism, it is believed that the God of Israel will one day give teḥiyyat ha-metim ("life to the dead") to the righteous during the messianic age, and they will live forever in the world at come (Olam Ha-Ba). The Jews base this belief on the Book of Isaiah (Yeshayahu), the Book of Ezekiel (Yeḥez'qel) and the Book of Daniel (Dani'el).

Ezekiel's vision:
The valley of dry bones,
engraving by Gustave Doré

COMMENTS

52. His disciples said to him:

"Twenty-four prophets spoke in Israel and all spoke through you. »

Jesus objects:

"You left the living in your presence and spoke about the dead. »

see CL 1:70, 1 JN 1, JN 1

The first question the reader has when reading these words is to ask himself, but who are these 24 prophets who spoke in Israel?

These 24 prophets are usually compared to the 24 elders found in the apocalypse of Saint John:

"And one of the elders said unto me, Weep not; behold, the lion of the tribe of Judah, the offspring of David, he overcame to open the book and its seven seals. And I saw, in the midst of the throne and of the four living creatures and in the midst of the elders, a lamb which was there as though slain. He had seven horns** and seven eyes, which are the seven spirits of God sent through all the earth. He came and took the book from the right hand of him who sat on the throne. When he had taken the book, the twenty-four elders prostrated themselves before the lamb, each holding a harp and golden bowls filled with incense, which are the prayers of the saints. And they sang a new song, saying, Worthy art thou to take the scroll, and to open its seals; for thou wast slain, and by thy blood thou hast redeemed men unto God out of every tribe, tongue, people, and nation. »*

* The four living beings are the drivers of the divine chariot, in the vision of Ezekiel 1, also called tetramorphs.

** Reference to the 7 horns of goats which served as trumpets to the Levites and which brought down the walls of Jericho (cf. Antiquities of the Jews, Book V).

In my opinion, the reference to the 24 prophets is a mnemonic and symbolic mean to remember the architecture of the Tanakh which symbolically represents a complete cycle similar to the twelve hours of the day and the twelve hours of the night. By this logion Jesus places himself at the origin of a new cycle and he defines himself moreover as a prophet.

For information, the Tanakh is divided into 3 large collections of books, the first section is called the Torah and was written by Moses, the second section is called Nevi'im and means the book of the prophets, finally the Tanakh ends with the Ketuvim which means the other writings.

The Trei Assar which is included in the Nevi'im, is commonly referred to as the Book of the 12 Minor Prophets. The 12 prophets in question are: Hosea, Joel, Amos, Obadiah, Jonah, Micah, Nahum, Habakkuk, Cepania, Haggai, Zechariah and Malachi. As authors of entire books, we find Moses (author of the Torah), Joshua, Samuel, Isaiah, Jeremiah, Ezekiel, David, Solomon, Job, Ruth, Esther, Daniel, Ezra and Nehemiah. If we remove the 2 women Ruth and Esther from this list, we find the figure of 24 which is made up of the 12 minor prophets who followed the 12 "great" prophets.

53. His disciples asked him:

"Is circumcision useful or not?

Jesus answered them:

If circumcision was useful then their fathers will have begot them circumcised from their mothers... But true circumcision, that of the spirit, is totally profitable. »

see RM 2, 1 COR 7, COL 2, GA 5, PH 3, EP 2.

It is no secret that Christian men are not circumcised. Christian tradition explains that this is due to the writings of Paul of Tarsus and if we refer to the Acts of the Apostles, we realize that the subject was extremely divisive and that it offended many people. So one wonders how Paul, on his own, managed to get across the idea that circumcision is unnecessary for Christians. How could he find the legitimacy and the reasons for such a speech?

The answer to these questions lies in this logion, where we understand that the Word of Jesus is at the origin of non-circumcision and that Paul was mainly his proselyte.

Finally, this logion testifies to the influence of Nazir teachings on the message of Jesus. Because the nazirs used the same argument for not cutting their hair, beard and nails while being circumcised by the spirit (asceticism).

COMMENTS

54. Jesus says:

***"Well-guided are the poors, the Kingdom of Heaven
is for you! »***

see MT 5, LK 6, JS 2, 1 TM 6

The parable of the poor is used several times by Jesus and it covers different meanings. Sometimes it means as in the present logon: asceticism. Sometimes it means as in the third logion: moral insufficiency.

As Luke will write later (12:21):

"So it is with him who lays up treasures for himself, and who is not rich for God. »

The idea that we also find in the Proverbs of Solomon (13: 7) is that material wealth leads away from spiritual wealth.

From a historical point of view, we know that part of the first Christian communities took the name of "poor". They are the ebionites and the name derives from the Hebrew ebyonim which means "the poor". These Judeo-Christians who recognized the messiahship of Jesus lived in roman Palestine in compliance with the laws of Moses, and had also spread to Cyprus, Syria, Rome, Persia and the Arabian Peninsula.

55. Jesus says:

"He who does not renounce his father and his mother cannot be my disciple. The one who does not renounce his brother and his sister and who does not take up his cross like me. This one will not become worthy of me."

see MT 10, LK 14, MK 8, MT 16: 24

Matthew, Mark and Luke, who are the authors of the synoptic gospels, situate this word when Jesus and his disciples traveled through the towns and villages of Israel. However, in my narrative sense as an editor, I find that this word would be placed very well during the martyrdom of Jesus in Jerusalem. When he was dragging his body on the cobblestones of the old town. When he carried the cross on his back, on the via dolorosa… When his relatives, seeing the horror, begged him to preserve his life by renouncing his faith.

The theme of dignity or to feel worthy to suffer offenses and outrages in the name of Jesus, is a theme that is found a lot in the writings of the authors of the New Testament. This confirms once again that the Word of Jesus contained in this collection had a very strong influence on the vision of the world of the apostles and disciples.

56. Jesus says:

"He who has understood the world, finds a corpse. Whoever found this corpse, the world is no longer worthy of him! »

see 1 Kings 13

One of the powers of the word of Jesus resides in his use of a colorful discourse. In one image, Jesus gives an explanation that has imperceptible depth and visible outline. Sometimes these images are lonely, sometimes they accompany his word until the end of the saying. Whether inert or animated, these parables decorate the words of Jesus with colors and smells...

In this logion, we discover the image of the corpse which in a single word conveys several meanings. In the image of a corpse, I see a body lying there, inert, dead, without a soul... a rotting body, stinking and foul... a lifeless and rigid body, left aside ready to be devoured by worms and scavengers. It is the image of death, and therefore of the one who is overcome by death, was devoured by the lion.

Whoever has understood the world discovers that this world is soulless and overcome by death. Whoever has understood that this world is overcome by horror, the world is no longer worthy of him.

57. Jesus says:

"The Kingdom of the Father is like a man who has good seeds to sow. At night his enemy came and sowed ryegrass among the good seed.

The man would not allow the ryegrass to be pulled up, lest, he said, in taking the ryegrass you would take away the wheat with them.

Indeed, on the day of harvest, the ryegrass will appear, they will be uprooted and burned! »

see MT 13, JL 3, AP 14

In Christian imagery, hell is where evil souls will be burned with fire. Doesn't this association with fire come from this word? Like the image of Satan with half-man and half-goat features, does it not come from the cult of Pan officiated at Caesarea Panias also called Caesarea Phillip?

In this work, I try to privilege the canonical Christian sources and not to dilute them with other sources of the Book descended in the name of God. The term day of harvest means both in the mouth of the prophet of Islam and in the writings of Matthew: the day of the last judgment. This shows the influence of the prophetic analyzes of the Word of Jesus made by Stephen, Phillip and the other Hellenist deacons.

58. Jesus says:

**"Blessed is the man who has been tried in his life,
because he entered into life. »**

see JS 1:12

Before studying the possible meanings of this logion, it should be noted that this logion confirms the free and independent use of the Words of Jesus by the authors of the New Testament.

To return to the meaning of this logion, what a sweet dream that of an easy life without trials or difficulties. However, those who live in ease and who are reluctant to make efforts encounter many difficulties in life. Because the one who has not known the test, the one who does not manage to surpass himself and to go even higher, that one has not known the meaning of life.

When I set out to follow the path of Virtue, I heard the crows of doom laughing at me. Walking this path seemed like a lonely and difficult journey, so against the grain of others. Yet today when I look behind me, I see them: sad, worried and hungry.

59. Jesus says:

"Turn your eyes towards the Living, as long as you are alive. Dead you will seek to see Him and you will no longer be able. »

see JN 16:16

Whether at school or on social networks, whether on the internet or in the street, we hear atheists making fun of believers. However, having discussed it with the oldest, the vast majority of them will change their minds before the end… When death comes, they will take fright and they will begin to believe.

This is why I prefer to see them as people who are waiting for understanding, rather than as people who have a firm opinion. Because he who is solid, remains so until the end…

So let us listen to Jesus' teaching and look to the Highest while we are alive, for when we are dead it will be too late to find the Place of Rest.

60.

Seeing a Samaritan carrying a lamb entering Judea, Jesus asked his disciples about the lamb.

They answered him: "He will kill him and eat him!" »

Jesus says, "He will not eat him while he is alive, but only if he kills him and he becomes a corpse. »

The disciples added: "For no other reason would he hurt him!" »

Then Jesus concludes: "You also, therefore, seek the Place of Rest, lest you become corpses, lest you be eaten. »

The Place of Rest is a term that will later become that of paradise. The term paradise comes from a very old language, Avestan Iranian, in which pairidaēza meant a royal or noble enclosure. The term is then transmitted to Persian in which pardēz means an enclosure. Then the term is transmitted to ancient Greek and will mean an enclosed park where wild animals are found. Finally, this term will slide towards Latin and will give the word paradisus. According to its first meaning in the Greco-Roman world, the term takes on with Christianization the meaning of celestial garden, namely the "garden or enclosure of Genesis". Reading the Fathers of the Church, such as Tertullian or Jerome of Stridon confirms the semantic tracing of Greek on Latin to designate both the garden given to Adam and Eve and the "abode of the just" in Heaven.

61. Jesus says:

"Two will rest on a bed,
one will die, the other will live.

Marie-Salome asked him: Who are you, man? Whose son are you? You climbed on my bed and you shared my table, yet I wonder. Who are you, man? Who were you born from?

Jesus answers her: I am the one who came from the one who remains constant. I have been given what comes from my Father.

Marie-Salome exclaimed: I am your disciple!

So Jesus concludes: "Because of this, I say this, when the disciple is open, he lets in the light and is filled with it.
But when he is divided, he is filled with darkness. »

see LK 17:34

It is because Jesus welcomes women into his community and gives them a legitimate place that Christian sisters have been able to take such an important place in Christianity, working like men to serve the community, through teaching or medicine, through their prayers and their devotions.

In this logion, women are made equal to men and they ask themselves the same questions (who are you, man?), they are also invited to make unity with the Light and to become disciples.

COMMENTS

62. Jesus says:

"I tell my mysteries to those who are worthy of my secrets. Let your left hand ignore what your right hand is working out. »

see MT 6, MT 13, MC 4:11, LK 8:10, MT 19:11

This first sentence: "I tell my mysteries to those who are worthy of my secrets. is magnetically eloquent. In front of such a word, one can only remain speechless and admiring, seduced by the mysterious, one would like to become worthy of its secrets.

The reader, like the disciples, hopes to hear from Jesus a simple and direct answer, yet, systematically, Jesus sends them back to themselves, if they wish to find the answer, they will have to learn to seek for themselves. This is how they will become adults. At best Jesus gives clues and in this logion the clue is to learn how to become worthy of him.

"Let your left hand ignore what your right hand is working out. is perhaps a reference to the Abrahamic imaginary where the right is synonymous with the good side of things and the left is synonymous with the bad side of things. From then on, we would get your bad side to ignore what your good side is preparing….Be vigilant!

63. Jesus says:

"There was a rich man who had a lot of wealth. He thought of using his fortune to sow the fields. When the harvest comes, he thought to himself, my barns will be full and I won't want for anything.

That same night he died.

Let him who has ears to hear, hear! »

see LK 12

The human being spends his life in search of wealth and this wealth makes him miss the essential. You don't need wealth to be happy, you don't need wealth to find love or have a family. No need for wealth to prepare for his death, because in the afterlife no one will take material wealth.

In the teaching of Jesus, his material quests are seen as distractions that prevent human beings from rising towards the spiritual, towards a world of sharing, love and unity.

The arrogant thinks he has everythig, but in fact, he lacks the essentials... With his eyes staring at the handlebars, this ignorant will crash into a wall. It's only a matter of time, he better figure it out before the end!

64. Jesus says:

"A man had guests, and when he had prepared the feast, he sent his servant to call those guests.

The servant went to the first guest and told him that his master was inviting him. He answered him:

I have money for merchants and they come to my house tonight and I have orders to place. I apologize for the feast.

The servant then went to another guest and told him that his master was calling him. He answered him:

I bought a house and it will take me all day. I am not free today, I apologize to your master.

The servant then went to another guest and told him that his master was calling him. He answered him:

My friend is getting married, and I am preparing the feast. Sorry, I couldn't come.

The servant then went to the last guest and told him that his master was waiting for him. He answered him:

I bought a field, and I have not yet gone to collect my share. I apologize for the feast, but I couldn't come.

The servant returned and told his master that those whom he had invited to the feast had apologized.

The master then said to his servant:

Go outside, in the streets, and those you find, bring them to me to dine. Buyers and merchants will not enter my Father's house. »

see MT 22, LK 14, MK 11

In this story of refusal and non-recognition, there is a lot to be learned. In the image of the feast or food, we should not see only material food, but above all spiritual food. Jesus and his disciples offered free spiritual and material food to men, women and children. The poor people heard his message, few were among the rich people who agreed to participate in his ministry.

The evangelists equated the image of "my Father's house" with the temple in Jerusalem, which was occupied by buyers and sellers of sacrifice. Concerning the light hidden behind the images of the master and the servant, the first possibility is that these images would represent Jesus as a servant and God as his master. Because in the New Testament Jesus is often referred to as the slave or the servant. Another possibility that seems consistent with the end of the logion is that they represent Jesus commissioning his disciples to preach the coming of the Kingdom.

There remains one last question for oneself: When a servant comes to propose to us to enter the Kingdom, will you be hungry to enter it?

65. Jesus says:

"A man of integrity had a vineyard which he had given to farmers to work on it and receive from them the fruit.

He sent his servant for the cultivators to give him the fruit of the vineyard. They seized his servant, struck him and nearly killed him.

The servant returned and told his master. His master thought, maybe they didn't recognize him?

He then sent another servant. This one also the cultivators struck him.

So the master sent his son, saying to himself that perhaps they would be ashamed to behave in this way with his child.

But, when the growers knew that this one was the heir to the vineyard. They seized him and killed him.

Let him who has ears to hear, hear! »

see MT 21, LK 20, MK 12

This word of Jesus pronounced before his martyrdom has bitter and prophetic flavors. Jesus knew what awaited him and with dignity he walked towards his disastrous destiny.

COMMENTS

66. Jesus says:

"Show me the stone that the builders rejected. This is the cornerstone. »

see MT 21, LK 20, MK 12, PS 118, JB 38, AC 4, EP 2, 1 P 2

This Parable was written by David in his Psalm 118. This affirmation has consensus among the evangelists since Matthew writes in chapter 21, verse 42:

"Jesus said to them: Have you never read in the Scriptures: the stone which the builders rejected has become the chief corner stone; it came from the Lord, And it is a wonder in our eyes? »

Peter and Paul of Tarsus explained in their epistles that it was Jesus Christ who was the cornerstone rejected by the builders. This interpretation is also that of Luke in the Acts of the Apostles:

"This Jesus is the stone rejected by you from the building, and which has become the cornerstone. »

There is in this logion a precept of vigilance to be observed, a certain precaution to be taken with people and things that seem unimportant, because as we do not know the future, it is possible that the stone which was rejected yesterday by the great leaders become more important and more visible than the builders.

67. Jesus says:

"He who knows everything, when he does not know himself, he is... deprived of everything. »

In this logion we find an idea that we find several times in this book. That of turning towards oneself, towards the interior of oneself, because this logion classifies the knowledge of oneself as more important than the knowledge of all that is outside of oneself. Good understanding therefore begins with oneself. Clairvoyance begins with knowing how to look at yourself precisely.

What is the point of knowing others if you don't know yourself? What's the point of knowing everything if you don't know yourself? He who is really solid, is solid in his head. If he needs others to be solid, then he is weak, because he depends on others...

68. Jesus says:

"Well-guided are those who are hated and persecuted. Those who persecute you will not find the place where they will not be persecuted. »

see MT 5, LK 6

It is a comforting word for those who are victims of hatred and persecution to know that in the end they will be rewarded for holding on.

Those who persecute and hate others to gain a sense of superiority do not realize that they are planting the seed of suffering in their hearts. Little by little the suffering will catch up with them, and the violence they have given, they will receive in return. A day will come when they will realize with regret their mistakes and they will realize the futility of having pursued illusions.

The place where they will not be persecuted is the place where they can rest eternally in safety, that is to say Peace. Those who hate and persecute will find neither on this earth nor in the afterlife: the Place of Rest.

69. Jesus says:

"Well-guided are those who have been persecuted in their hearts. These are the ones in truth who have known the Father. Well-guided are those who are hungry, they can satisfy the belly of whoever wants.»

see MT 5, LK 6

These last two logions are often compared with the Beatitudes of the Gospel according to Matthew and the Gospel according to Luke. Their anaphoric style as well as their contents go in any case in this direction.

To return to the meaning of these words, those who are persecuted in their beings and in their beliefs must not renounce their faith, although this may seem to go against the current of events. The noble life and the great truth come after facing trials. Without trials, life and truth are not believable. This message, which brings comfort and certainty, pushes the human being to remain solid and to continue to move forward despite the difficulties.

Well-guided are those who hunger for knowledge and success. By their work, they will make the fields fruitful and will have enough to feed everyone. The parable of hunger should not be taken in the strict sense of the word, but should also be understood as this force that strives all living beings in motion: to be hungry to live, to be hungry to enter the Kingdom, to be hungry to know and to succeed i.e. to pass the tests.

70. Jesus says:

"When it is begotten in you, it will save you. But if you haven't got it in you, it'll kill you. »

In its original format, this book does not contain any context or background. It also contains no explanations and the interpretation of the Words of Jesus is left to the reader. With this logion, we glimpse the problems of interpretations posed by this work and which are at the origin of the writing of the Gospels and their Gnostic counterparts. Because who can say with certainty what "it" is?

According to Jesus' formulation, "it" is a thing of extreme importance, because it will save you and its absence will kill you. So what is it? Is it faith? Is it God? Is this life? Is it teaching? Is it Virtue or a higher state of consciousness? This single word of "it" can be replaced by a multitude of other words that would allow the sentence to have a clearer meaning.

The meaning of "it" is most mysterious and the main effect of this word is to invite its listener or its reader to seek to know what it is. And perhaps it is the purpose of this logion.

71. Jesus says:

"I will tear down this house, and no one can rebuild it. »

see MT 26, MK 14, JN 2, AC 6

For John the Evangelist, the house in question is the body of Jesus. For Matthew, Mark and Luke, this word concerns the temple in Jerusalem. My interpretation is that the house in question represents the line of Sadducean priests. Because the temple on Mount Temple has been rebuilt but the line of Sadducees is over.

The prophetic interpretation that the house in question is the temple of Jerusalem was at the origin of the martyrdom of Saint Stephen and we find its mention in the Acts of the Apostles whenever it is said that the apostles preached against this location. Similarly, when it is written that the apostles preach against the laws of Moses, we must see the reference to logion 53. These two logions, 71 and 53, are the 2 main points of tension between Christians and Pharisees. During the mandate of James-the-Just, the Judeo-Christians will propose interpretations which do not tense the resentment of the Jews. This is the interpretation that John takes up concerning the house and it is also the importance of the word indispensable in the apostolic letter. It means that for the Jews, circumcision is an indispensable act. Therefore the Jews who recognize in Jesus: the Christ, must continue to circumcise themselves.

72. A man called out to Jesus:

"Speak to my brothers so that they share with me the property of my father.

Jesus answers him: Tell me, man, who has made me a sharer?

He turned to his disciples and said to them: Am I really a divider? »

see LK 12

If one refers to the Acts of the Apostles as well as to the Dead Sea Scrolls, Essene economic life resembled to a communist sharing system, so by entering the community, one gave everything that one had to his representative (the bishop) who had the charge of providing for the needs of his members.

Therefore, we understand Jesus' response, which promotes the unity that the Essene sharing brings. Conversely, he does not believe in sharing which leads to a division of property.

A collectivist system of sharing is still found today among the Jews of Israel, in what are commonly called kibbutzim. The Kibbutz are independent communities which live together in a delimited territory and which share the common fruit of their labor equally among their members. Similarly, the Kibbouz community is responsible for meeting the needs of its members.

73. Jesus says:

"The harvest is plentiful. Few are the workers. Pray to the Lord to send workers into the harvest. »

see MT 9, LK 10

This logion prefigures the office of prayer in Christianity. Prayer is not used solely as an expression of blessing or praise. Nor does it serve to be forgiven or as a lament. But it is also used to call for a benefit.

In the Our Father, which is the most widespread Christian prayer, because it was taught by Jesus to his disciples in the Gospels, the Christian first calls for the coming of the Kingdom, then to be nourished, finally to be forgiven and well guided. Thus he calls for a benefit.

The prayer was also used as a cement of Christian identity. The first Christian communities will develop thereafter towards a solitary and personal use. The fact that it is possible to use it to ask for a benefit is a novelty compared to the Jewish prayer which is carried out according to a calendar and a precise chronology as a sign of gratitude and praise.

74. Jesus said:

"Lord, many are standing around the well, but there is no one to go down. »

The meaning of this logion seems quite obvious, Jesus invites his listener to make the effort to get to the bottom of things, even if it is difficult. If we refer to the writings of Origen, one of the fathers of the Christian Church, this logion was found in an early Christian text called The Celestial Dialogue. Below is the excerpt from Contra Celse, Book VIII:

"As Celsus falsely imputes to us, the one to whom we now call the name Father. Here is how he talks about it in the sequel. To show that I am not deviating from the goal in proposing their belief, I will use their own words, as I have taken them from a certain dialogue which they call the Celestial Dialogue, where they express themselves in these terms: "If the Son of God is more powerful than his Father, and yet he himself is subject to the Son of man, who other than the latter can be master to the God who governs the world? How is it that there are so many people on the edge of the well and no one goes down? Why, after having come so far, do you lack courage here? You are wrong, replies the other, for I have courage and a sword. Doesn't it appear from this that their design is such as I have represented it? They suppose that there is another God above the two, who is the Father of him whom they worship with one accord; and in this way, under the pretext of serving the great God, they serve only this Son of man whom they have taken for their patron, and who is, they say, the master of the God who governs the world, being more powerful than him. This is why they

<u>recommend so carefully not to serve two masters</u>, so that their spirit of cabal has no other object than that alone. »

The text named the Celestial Dialogue has not been found and the fact that it has not been found combined with the little that is known of this writing suggests that it was a Gnostic writing.

What is interesting from an analytical point of view in this logion is that it is possible to link the collection of the Words of Jesus to both Gnostic writings and canonical scriptures. This confirms, moreover, that this work was considered authentic by both the Gnostics and the Canons. Because otherwise why would they have taken it up and tried to interpret it?

75. Jesus says:

"Many stand before the door, but it is the bachelors who will enter the bridal chamber. »

see JL 1, JL 2, MT 9, MK 2, LK 5, LK 13, JN 10

This word of Jesus was not taken up as such in the New Testament, however, there are two images that have been taken up separately. These are the image of the bridal chamber and that of the door. The bridal chamber represents the Place of Rest and also the place of union. Prosaically, the celibate is the one who seeks to unite and who will achieve unity in the nuptial chamber. To access it, he will have to go through the door.

According to John, it is Jesus who is the door, he is the means of entering the nuptial chamber, i.e a point of passage.

To explain this translation, the word that I have translated here by bachelor/celibate is actually the recurring Coptic word: monachos. A word which is also found in logions 23 and 48, and which I previously translated as one and united. This word comes from ancient Greek and its root, "monos", means the one who is alone, unique, in one piece.

76. Jesus says:

"The Kingdom of the Father is like a merchant who owned a cargo.

One day he came across a pearl. This merchant was wise. He decided to sell his merchandise and buy this unique pearl for himself.

You too, seek for yourselves this treasure which lasts and does not perish. Who resides where the moth does not approach, where the worm does not gnaw. »

see MT 13, IS 51, AC 12:23, MK 9:48,

The image of the pearl and the merchant might be a reference to the writings of Solomon. In his book of Proverbs, we find several times the image of the pearl associated with wisdom, these are chapters 3, 8, 21 and 30. In his figurative verb, wisdom represents greater wealth than the pearl, because it is an imperishable treasure while the pearl attracts lust, no one is jealous of it, no one can steal a well-earned wisdom. It is a treasure that will make you rich, happy and clairvoyant. It is a wealth that stands far beyond skill and intelligence...

If we refer to another important book of the Tanakh which tells the story of Solomon, i.e. The books of the Kings, Solomon spent the fortune he made with the merchants, to build in Jerusalem the first temple of the Jews as well as the royal palace and its protective walls.

77. Jesus says:

"I am the light which is above them all.

I am everything.
The whole came to me
The whole came out of me.

Split the wood, I'm here!
Lift a stone, you'll find me there! »

See PR 4:18, JN 1, JN 12, JN 8:12, 3:31,
EP 4:6, RM 11:36, 1CO 8:6

This logion is, in my opinion, one of the most important, because it is the concretization of the border which separates the canonicals from the gnostics. The image of Jesus as the light of the world has been taken up many times by Christian authors, while the rest of this logion has not been taken up in canonical writings. The Gnostics are characterized apart from an incomprehensible writing by a syncretic will which is an unsuccessful attempt at universalism. Historians do not explain the origin of this syncretism, nor the reasons which pushed this current of thought to go in this direction which is a mixture of almost everything.

My personal belief is that it was this logion that was behind their ill-fated attempt. My interpretation is that by his words, Jesus expresses the fact that he has reached a supreme level of consciousness which allows him to feel like, to understand, everything.

78. Jesus says:

*"What are your reasons for walking in the
countryside?*

*Is it to see a reed shaken by the wind?
Is it to observe a man wrapped in rich fabrics?*

*The kings and the powerful may wear beautiful
clothes on them, nevertheless they do not know
the truth ! »*

see MT 11, LK 7

This logion was taken up by Luke and Matthew in an almost identical way, but with differences on the adjectives and an absent end. This confirms the idea that the said Gospel of Thomas is an original document, because that is what is expected of documents deriving from an original text, we expect the transcription to be slightly different, we also expect that the themes and ideas they contain are developed to explain their meaning. This functioning is a natural process.

Finally, to come back to the meaning of this logion, it must be placed within the framework of Jesus' teaching to his disciples. And I think it should be put in parallel with logions 14 and 73.

79.
In the crowd, a woman called out to Jesus and said to him:

"Blessed is the belly that carried you.
Blessed is the breast that fed you!

Jesus answered him:

"Blessed are those who have heard the word of the Father and who keep it!
Verily, the days will come when you will say: 'Blessed were the days when this womb had not given birth, Blessed were the days when these breasts had not nursed! '"

see LK 11, PS 119: 1-2

This logion as well as logion 99 are the only direct and indirect references to Mary, the mother of Jesus. In the case of this logion, a woman in the crowd calls out to Jesus and professes to bless her mother and speaks of her as being blessed, i.e. worthy to enter the Kingdom.

Jesus replies that those who are promised to enter will be those who hear and keep the Word of the Father.

Obviously Jesus has already heard women talk about being happy. Knowing their reflections, Jesus adroitly reminds them that to be blessed is not to give birth or to keep the body of one's youth...

80. Jesus says:

**"He who understood this world, found the body.
Whoever found this body, for him, this world is no
longer worthy. »**

This logion is reminiscent in its structure of logion 56 and the only thing that differentiates them is the word body/flesh which replaces that of corpse. In the previous logion we had the word corpse which represented the image of death, in this logion we have the body which represents carnal impulses and desires, human bestiality, uncontrolled behavior.

These two parallel logions reveal the sad and pessimistic vision that Jesus has of the world. Because the world is associated with death and bestiality while the celestial Kingdom is associated with immortality and spiritual height.

There is in this speech which defines the world as unworthy, a perceptible disappointment and a buried melancholy. As if, deep down, Jesus wanted to get rid of his carnal envelope and let his spirit soar to the Kingdom of Heaven.

"He who understood this world, found the body. Whoever found this body, for him, this world is no longer worthy. »

81. Jesus said:

"Whoever has become rich, let him become king, and whoever has power, let him give it up. ".

This logion was not taken up clearly and literally in the New Testament, however, if you look closely, we find the reference to the theme of this logion, in the first epistle to the Corinthians by Paul of Tarsus (1 CO 4: 8):

"You are already satisfied, you are already rich, without us you have begun to reign. And may you indeed reign, so that we too may reign with you! »

In the Gospel of Matthew (MT 19:21):

"If you want to be perfect, go, sell what you have, give it to the poor, and you will have treasure in heaven. Then come, and follow me. »

And in the Gospel of Luke (LC 12:33):

"Sell what you have, and give it away in alms. Make yourself purses that do not wear out, an inexhaustible treasure in the heavens, where the thief does not approach, and where moth does not destroy. »

In the three references mentioned above, we notice that the theme of wealth and its counterpart of poverty, are not always to be understood only in a material sense, but that they are also to be understood in a spiritual sense. In the closing of his word, Jesus speaks to us of a high ascetic moral value : the virtue of renunciation.

82. Jesus says:

"He who is near me is near the fire. He who is far from me is far from the Kingdom. »

see MT 3:11, MK 12:34, LK 12:49

In this logion we find the image of fire which conveys, among other things, feelings of warmth, protection and light. This image is associated directly with Jesus, because according to the canonical gospels, Jesus is baptizing with the fire of the saintly spirit.

In the Jewish imagination, this fire of which Jesus speaks also recalls the divine fire which does not burn the burning bush. It means the divine voice which spoke to Moses, which commissioned him to bring out of Egypt, the children of Israel.

In the Jewish tradition, there is an important religious festival which is that of lights. It is in Hebrew Hanukkah, during this festival, the Jews meet every evening for 8 days and they light a candle every evening from their very particular candlabrum. The holiday ends when all 8 candles have been lit. On this candlabrum with 9 branches, there is a ninth candle which is used to light the 8 others and which is called: shamash, the servant...

83. Jesus says:

"Images reveal something to man, but the light that is in these images is hidden.

In the image of the Father, the image will reveal itself hidden by the light..."

see COL 1: 15-17

In this logion, Jesus teaches us what to understand in his use of images. The image cannot fully render the meaning of his idea and you have to look behind the image for the meaning he wishes to give. The image gives an outline to a thing that has no outline, which is why it speaks of light, which in essence is elusive and without outline.

Throughout this collection of the Words of Jesus as well as in the New Testament, the term comes up constantly, sometimes it is translated by icons or model, sometimes it is translated by the word parable. In any case, it must be understood that this colorful discourse characterizes Jesus.

84. Jesus says:

"For whole days you stare at your reflection and rejoice.

But, when you see your models, those who came into existence long before you, those who no longer die and no longer manifest.

How long will you endure it? »

see 2CO3: 18

<u>No comment.</u>

85. Jesus says:

"Adam came into existence out of great power and great wealth.

Yet he was not deemed worthy of you. If he had been deemed worthy, he would not have tasted death. »

see HE 3: 3, HE 6: 4-8

This logion testifies to the right position of Jesus towards women. In a very skilful way, Jesus enlightens us on his understanding of the so-called original sin.

According to Jewish tradition derived from the Torah, Adam's fault when he ate the fruit of knowledge was due to his wife Eve. It is she who convinces Adam to taste it and when Adam bites into the forbidden fruit, he lost eternal life.

In this logion Jesus implies that Adam's fault is mainly due to himself. Eve did not force him, Adam is responsible for his choice which led to the loss of his dignity. His responsibility is all the greater because he was born out of great power and great wealth.

86. Jesus says:

"Foxes have dens. Birds have nests. Yet the son of man has no place on earth to lay his head and rest. »

see MT 8, LK 9

Logions 3, 8, 86 and 90 all relate to animals and in all these logions animals are placed closer than human beings to the Kingdom of God. These logions testify that Jesus had a high opinion of the value of an animal life.

Animals have found on earth the Place to rest. The son of man did not find among men the means to live in peace on earth. He seeks the Place of Rest in the Kingdom of Heaven.

87. Jesus says:

"Wretched is the body that depends on another body. Unhappy is the soul that depends on these two. »

The well-guided or happy way is the one that is neither unhappy nor miserable. The miserable path is the one that should not be followed, while the well-guided path represents the true path.

Jesus teaches us, in this lodge, not to follow the path of dependency. Because it is a harmful soil that will not lead to the harvest of good fruit.

The happy and true path speaks of Unity, Love and Liberation. By the way, we get:

Happy is the body that unites with another body.
Joyful is the soul that unites these two.

Happy is the body that loves another body.
Joyful is the soul that loves these two.

Happy is the body that frees itself from another body.
Joyful is the soul that frees itself from these two.

88. Jesus says:

"The angels come with the prophets to give you what is yours.
Yourselves, give them what you have and ask yourselves:

What day will they come to take what is theirs? »

When will you give back to God?

What belongs to Him?

89. Jesus says:

"Why do you only wash the outside of the cup?

Don't you understand then that he who created the outer side also created the inner side? »

see MT 23:26, LK 11:39-40

Seek and you will find...

90. Jesus said:

"Come to me, my yoke is just. Sweet is my authority and you will find (eternal) rest for yourselves. »*

** The yoke is a piece of wood that is put on the heads of oxen in order to hitch them up and guide them.*

see MT 11

This logion is one of the few logions where Jesus speaks in the first person and which presumably expresses the bottom of his feelings, the logions concerned are: 13, 17, 23, 28, 30, 61, 71, 77, 90 and 108.

In this logion, Jesus expresses his conception of his government. He does not conceive of him as an authoritarian who would wave a stick to guide the animal. Nor does he conceive of it as a hindrance that would symbolize the submission of the animal.

On the contrary, Jesus presents himself as a loving guide to his people. He is the farmer who loves his beef and respects it. He does not want him to exhaust himself with the task and die of fatigue. He brings him security and well-being and it is because he has put his yoke on the ox that it is protected from sacrifice.

In return for its benefits, the ox allows itself to be guided and plows the earth better than a hundred people. It is with justice that he guides, it is with gentleness that he convinces.

91. They said to him:

"Tell us who you are, so that we believe in you. »

Jesus replies:

You scrutinize the aspect of heaven and earth, but the one in front of you you do not recognize. This present moment you do not know how to interpret. »

see MT 16:2-3, LK 12:56

<u>No comment.</u>

92. Jesus says:

"Seek and you will find! The things about which you had asked me and which in those days I had not told you. Now I wish to tell you, but you no longer seek it.
»

see JN 16:4

Perhaps if the disciples no longer seek or no longer need to hear Jesus says, it is because they have found who Jesus is. From then on they no longer look to know who he is, they have recognized him...

93.

*"Don't give what is holy to dogs or it will end up like manure. Do not throw the pearls to the pigs lest they make... *"*

**The word is incomplete on the Coptic manuscript of Nag-Hammadi.*

see MT 7

Like many men, I have tried to give what is holy and wise to those who are foolish or unwilling to hear. What results has unfortunately not changed in 2000 years...

94. Jesus says:

"Whoever seeks will find, to whoever wishes to enter, the door will be opened. »

see MT 7, LC 11

Through his universalist message, Jesus opens the doors of the Kingdom to everyone, whether you are a man or a woman, whether you are a child or an old person, whether you are rich or poor, whether one is a Jew or a foreigner: to whoever wishes to enter, the door will be opened. The only constraint is to look for it during his lifetime.

95. *Jesus says:*

"*If you have money, do not lend it with interest, but give it to he who has nothing in his hands. »*

see MT 5:42, MT 19:21, DT 23:19, EX 22:25*

In all the logions that concern Jesus and his relationship with money, we see that he is not in search of material wealth. Rather than locking ourselves into a desire for greed, or accumulating money without limits at the expense of others, let's give it to those who really need it. In the continuity of an ascetic message in favor of the practice of almsgiving and renunciation, Jesus teaches us to show sharing towards the poor and the brothers*.

96. *Jesus says:*

"*The Kingdom of the Father is like a woman who has hidden a little leaven in her flour. The dough grows slowly and will form beautiful loaves.*

Let him who has ears to hear, hear! »*

see MT 13, LK 13, 1 CO 5, MT 16: 6, MC 8: 15, GA 5: 9

The image of leaven hides the sense of belief. By this analogy, Jesus shows us his importance and his reward.

97. Jesus says:

"The Kingdom of the Father is like a woman who bears a vessel full of fruit. She goes along the path and on the road, the handle of the vase breaks and the fruits spill out behind her. The woman does not know or care. When she got home. She puts the vase down, turns it over and finds it empty! »

see LC 7:36-39, MC 14:3, MT 26:7

In these two consecutives logions, the image of the father is compared to the image of a woman… The fruits she bears are surely those of knowledge and they spread behind it. When she returns to her house, she realizes that she has left everything behind.

The strength of Jesus' message is its inexhaustible interpretation, which is matched only by the sum of what is left unsaid. In this parable, the disciple who hears the story is also the observer. Understanding the importance of his teaching, he goes in search of the fruits and when he has found them all, what will he do? Should he keep them for himself? Should he return them to the owner?

Because, when you have found everything, there is nothing more to look for. When you have understood everything, there is nothing more to understand. When you have done everything, there is nothing more to do. This, in my opinion, is the reason for the silence and inaction of the Eternal. He is waiting for us…

98. Jesus says:

"The Kingdom of the Father is like a man who wants to kill a powerful man. In his house, he draws the sword and sticks it in a wall. Once he makes sure his hand is steady, he kills the man of power. »

No comment.

99. The disciples said to him:

"Outside are your brothers and your mother!"

He answered them,

You and those who do my Father's will, these are my brothers and my mother. They are the ones who will come into my Father's kingdom. "

see MT 12, MK 3, LK 8

Seek and you will find!

100.

*They showed Jesus a gold coin stamped with
Caesar's face and said to him:*

"Caesar's men are asking us to pay their taxes.

*Jesus answered: Give Caesar what is Caesar's.
Give to God what is God's.
And what is mine, give it to me! »*

see MT 22, MK 12, LK 20

This Word of Jesus has become over time one of the most famous. In this logion we perceive the pacifist values of Jesus, because at that time the Jews intimately hoped for the arrival of a messiah who, like Moses, would deliver them from the yoke of the Romans. Implicitly, some Jews therefore ask him whether he intends to fight against the romans taxation. Because, for the Jews, the act of submission is being manifested by the tax they had to pay to the romans.

From the previous logions, we know Jesus' relationship with money, which is why his answer is in accordance to his teaching. Jesus leaves aside the material and he glorifies the spiritual, what he asks is to be given what is his : the government of the Kingdom.

COMMENTS

101.

"He who does not renounce his father and his mother, as I did. This one cannot become my disciple.

The one who does not love his father and his mother, as I did. This one cannot become my disciple.

Because my mother gave me a body to die, but my true mother gave me life. »

see CM 10: 29-30, LK 18: 29-30, MT 10: 37-39

In this logion the image of the Father merges with that of a Mother. We therefore understand that these are images that give shape to a background of unfathomable depth.

Through this logion, Jesus shares with us his intellectual journey and the steps he had to take in his life to get where he is. It is very rare that Jesus speaks about himself and when he does it is in a subtle way. According to these words, Jesus succeeds in freeing himself from his parents without, however, ceasing to love them deeply. His mother gave him a body, it is true, but it was the Lord who sent the spirit upon him and breathed into him this new life.

From a thematic point of view, we find in this word, the values of love and renunciation. We also find the expression of his deep gratitude to the Eternal.

102. Jesus said:

"Woe to them, woe to these Pharisees! They look like a dog lying down in the cattle manger. He neither eats this food nor does he let the oxen eat. »

see MT 23

We had previously spoken of the classification between the happy path and the miserable path. Jesus in this logion which is addressed to the Pharisee elites speaks of an intermediate way which he defines as unfortunate. This way is unfortunate, because it is incomplete compared to the happy way, i.e. that it does not give fullness. By hiding the priceless, they prevent believers from fully and freely obtaining what they seek.

This logion, which will be taken up and amplified by Matthew, denotes the deep divisions that separated the Jewish communities from each other. And chapter 23 of Matthew gives the philosophical and theological explanation, because the origin of the fracture lies in the weight of traditions from the Torah. The Pharisees wanted to fix the laws of Moses and make them permanent and unchangeable.

This conservative vision will be upset by the fall of the Temple and as surprising as it may seem, it is thanks to this event that the Pharisees succeeded in sanctifying Judaism and regaining its unity. Finally, it is the starting point of the age-old debates of the rabbis: the Talmud.

103. Jesus says:

"Blessed is the man who knows when the thieves are coming. Let him watch and gather his wealth and family, arm himself before they enter. »

see MT 24, LK 12, 2P 3: 10, AP 3: 2-3, AP 16: 15

This logion can be interpreted in two ways: in a wise way and in an apocalyptic way.

According to an interpretation based on a message of wisdom, Jesus teaches us to be vigilant and to be ready in the face of death.

From an apocalyptic perspective, this logion is about doomsday. Knowing that the day is coming, they must be vigilant and be ready.

According to the study of the New Testament, it was the apocalyptic interpretation that was favored by the first Christians.

104. They said:

"Come, let us pray and fast today.

Jesus replies:

*What is this sin that I have committed?
How did they conquer me?*

*But it is when the spouse has left the marital room
that it is necessary to fast and pray. »*

see MT 9: 14-15, MK 2: 18-20, LK 5: 33-35

Prayer and fasting should serve for the remission of sins, they should not be used lightly. Because as Jesus concludes, it is when the husband will have sinned by cheating on his wife, that he will seek to purify himself through fasting or prayer. It is when the husband will have been conquered by his carnal desires, that he will seek to purify himself through fasting and prayer.

COMMENTS

105. Jesus says:

**"He who knows his father and his mother,
would they call him the son of a prostitute? »**

At first I wanted to leave this logion uncommented and then I thought there was an interesting commentary about it that confirms that this book is where the right and wrong interpretation comes from. How it served for its defenders to glorify it and how it served for its detractors to infamous it. Because this logion certainly served as a base for the calumny which tells that Jesus is the illegitimate son that his mother would have had with a roman soldier named Pantera. By this unfounded rumor, it is the dishonor that is thrown on his mother who is compared to a prostitute and it is the defilement that is thrown on his son Jesus who is compared to a bastard.

This rhetorical means which consists in weakening the arguments of its detractor by the personal lowering of its speaker is in my opinion, the weapon of the weak and irresponsible. By smearing their opponent, they think they are rising above him and it must be recognized that this degrading technique has a certain result with the ignorants. For my part, the one who demonstrates this technique inspires me with disgust and his aura lowers.

A politician had thus explained the tactic: when you have no argument to counter your interlocutor, the last you can do is to tarnish his image in front of others…

COMMENTS

106. Jesus says:

"When you unite the two into one,
you will become the sons of men
and if you say to the mountain,
go away, then she will go away. »

see MT 17, MK 11, LK 17

This logion is to be compared with logion 48. By their syntaxes and their contents, these logions seem similar and imply the same consequence: the mountain will move away.

While Logion 48 emphasized Peace, this present Logion emphasizes the unity or wholeness. Jesus said earlier that through peace, human beings will be able to unite opposites. By doing the union in oneself, the human being is able to reach the whole plenitude.

One who has reached this supreme state of consciousness will become impeccable and will be compared to the biblical son of man. For him, there will be nothing insurmountable that cannot be overcome.

107. Jesus says:

*"The Kingdom is like a shepherd who had a hundred
sheep. One of them, the largest, got lost.
The shepherd left the other ninety-nine and went after
her until he found her.
After being tested, he said to the sheep:
I love you more than the other ninety-nine"*

see MT 18, LK 15, MT 15: 24, 1 P 2: 25, PS 23

The parable of the shepherd or pastor was widely taken up by early Christian and pseudo-Christian content publishers. The simplicity of the image which speaks to all as well as the message of love of Jesus towards the astray, explain this perpetual appropriation which will become in the Gospel of John, one of the major words of his book. This logion also makes use of a parable from the psalm of David in which God is the shepherd.

To come back to the meaning of this logion, if the sheep escaped from the herd when it was safe there, it was probably because she did not feel in its place. It's probably because she didn't feel loved or recognition. Understanding this, the shepherd goes to her and shows her his love so that she feels reassured with him. According to the teaching of Jesus, this is a peaceful way to convince those who are lost and who are called astray. Their fate is therefore not final, because it is possible by the expression of a universal love to make them join the flock of the Eternal.

108. Jesus says:

*"Whoever drinks from my mouth will walk in my way.
I too will become like him and what is hidden will be
revealed to him. »*

see JN 7:37, IS 59:20-21, PR 18:14, PS 40:3, MT 26:30

109. Jesus says:

*"The Kingdom is like a man who has a hidden
treasure in his field and yet does not know it.*

*He did not find it before he died, and he left his field
to his son who also did not know that. He took the
field and he sold it.*

*Whoever bought it, plowed the field and found the
treasure. With this treasure, he began to lend at
interest to whoever wants it. »*

see MT 13

110. Jesus says:

*"He who has found the world and made himself rich,
let him renounce this world. »*

see MT 19:21, LC 18:22, CA 4:34

These three logions address themes already
explored previously. The repetition of the themes
shows that these words come from one and the same
person. This collection is therefore authentic.

111. Jesus says:

*"The heavens and the earth will roll up before you,
and he who lives of the living will not see death.
That is why I say: he who finds himself, the world is
not worthy of him. »*

see MT 24:35, MC 13:31, LC 21:33, IS 51:6

This logion can be analyzed through an apocalyptic vision and in this case, it seems to refer to the day of the last judgment and the return of Jesus at its fulfillment.

Concerning the second part of this logion, it is interesting to keep in mind that we can often analyze the words of a person with regard to their personal experience. In this case, with regard to his teaching, we are entitled to understand that Jesus found himself to be a child of the Light and that when he understood this, he realized that in this world: rare are the sons of Light and many are the sons of darkness...

112. Jesus said:

*"Wretched is the flesh that depends on the soul.
Wretched is the soul that depends on the flesh. »*

This logion, which speaks again of the wretched way, is of a structure similar to logion 87. While the previous logion spoke of the danger of an external dependence, this one speaks of the danger of an internal dependence. Jesus advocates a just and complete unity of flesh and soul, without a state of dependence.

113. The disciples asked him:

"What will be the day of the coming of the Kingdom?

Jesus replies:

He does not come looking outward. People won't say look he's here, see he's over there.

The Kingdom of the Father is spreading over the earth and men do not see it. »

see LC 17, MT 24: 3, CA 1: 6-8

The theme of the Kingdom of God is one of the major themes of Jesus' message and it is also the one that fascinates the disciples. This is why to Jesus who found himself, the disciples ask him when will the Kingdom of God descend on Earth. Accurately and appropriately, Jesus answers them that the Kingdom begins within oneself and that its realization has already begun since the disciples have received his teaching... Even if people do not yet see the Kingdom is coming, it will come.

Understanding this, disciples will follow the teachings of Logions 14 and 73 and begin their apostolic mission in which they will be charged with bringing down the Kingdom of Heaven to Earth.

114. Simon Peter says:

"Let Mary Magdalene come out of our midst, for women are not worthy of life.

Jesus says:

Listen, I will guide her so that she becomes a man. Thus it will become a breath of life resembling you men.

For every woman who becomes a man will enter the Kingdom of Heaven. »

This final logion shows that the arrival of women and in particular that of Mary Magdalene among the relatives is difficult to accept by the disciples. Peter makes himself the voice of the whispers. In the Jewish culture of the first century AD, women were excluded from philosophical debate. Considered as impure and despised, because guilty of pulling men away from God, they had a place that frankly did not enhance them. In the Essene culture, the position of men towards women was even more vindictive and women not only found themselves figuratively excluded from theological debate, but this time found themselves physically excluded from the community.

In this final logion, Jesus abolishes this rule and by his wprd puts women on the same level as men. They are equal to men and they too will enter the Kingdom when they have united their masculine and feminine sides into one noble and happy

<u>*Unity*</u>

With God
With oneself
With others
With Earth
With Universe

Join us on :

À PARAÎTRE

FORTHCOMING

From Ahl al-Kitab editions

Proverbes of Salomon

The Analects of Confucius

Bhagavad-Gita of Krishna

Muhammad's Quran

ALREADY PUBLISHED

Dhammapada of Siddhartha Gautama

Tao Te King of Lao-zi

The Gospel of Thomas, Q source of Christainity